STEP-BY-STEP
CONSTRUCTIVE
BIDDING

Tony Sowter

STEP-BY-STEP CONSTRUCTIVE BIDDING

B. T. Batsford Ltd, *London*

First published 1994

© Tony Sowter 1994

ISBN 0 7134 7639 7

A CIP catalogue record for this book is available from the British Library.

Typeset by Apsbridge Services Ltd, Nottingham.
Printed by Redwood Books, Trowbridge, Wiltshire
for the publishers,
B. T. Batsford Ltd, 4 Fitzhardinge Street,
London W1H 0AH

A BATSFORD BRIDGE BOOK
Series Editor: Tony Sowter

CONTENTS

INTRODUCTION

Without any doubt, the content of this book has been inspired by the countless hours that I have enjoyed both teaching and discussing the principles of natural bidding in my bridge classes. Unlike most bridge teachers, I cannot claim that I have spent many years introducing new players into the game, preferring, instead, to spend my time quenching the thirst of the many keen, established players who want to improve their game.

Step by Step: Constructive Bidding is not aimed at either the beginner or the expert bridge player. Instead, it is aimed at the many thousands of players who might be described as fairly experienced, average players. Most players in this category have learned their bridge either from their friends or by attending one or two courses of beginners lessons. After that, it is all down to the scraps of information garnered at the local club or the lessons learned from losing the occasional friendly rubber. All too often there are enormous gaps in the player's knowledge of basic bidding theory and, worse still, a total reliance on rules which were driven home in those early lessons in order to get them started.

I hope that this book addresses most, if not all, of those issues – and, hopefully, in a way that helps you both to understand the principles involved and to learn them. To this end, you will find that each chapter starts off addressing one or two major issues and then you are faced with a series of bidding problems, which I hope will serve to drive the point home as well as illustrating a few other principles that apply in each area. In order for you to get the most out of this book, I strongly urge you to force yourself to write your own answers to each quiz down on a separate piece of paper before reading the answers and explanations in this text. Equally important, if you are sharing this book with your partner, make sure that you answer the questions separately. By all means, compare notes afterwards but rely on your own bidding judgement first.

Over the years, I have played all sorts of systems, strong 1♣ systems, strong 2♣ systems, four card majors and five card majors and even a variable forcing pass system at international level. However, at the end of the day, I am most at home playing a natural, four card major system.

Without doubt, in the world of bridge at the moment, five card majors hold sway. In the past twenty years, the theory of bidding after a five card major opening has advanced rapidly; however, whatever the advantage is of knowing that when partner opens 1♡ or 1♠ he has a least five of them, in my view it is largely negated by the need to open with either a prepared 1♣ or a prepared 1♢ or even both.

While four card major systems do not suffer in quite the same way from this disadvantage, all too often four card major players fail to exploit the natural advantages of opening four card majors. Believe me, in the competitive situation, it is a great advantage to be opening one of a major more frequently. It is a lot harder for your opponents to get into the bidding if you open 1♡ or 1♠ than if you open 1♣ or 1♢, and your opponents' problems are compounded if your partner can raise you as high and as frequently as possible.

Of course, this book is not about competitive bidding but, in order to extract the maximum competitive advantage from playing four card majors, you need a sound basis to your system. I hope that this book will help to provide it for you.

As the editor of the new series of Batsford Bridge books, I am particularly pleased to have had the opportunity to write one of the first titles in the Step by Step series, which I hope you will enjoy.

Tony Sowter
May, 1994

1
OPENING THE BIDDING

It may seem strange to start with an example; however, when the following deal occurred, it struck me as being an excellent illustration of one of the major problems encountered by many average players day after day.

Playing in a teams competition, you find yourself holding this hand:

♠ AK52
♡ 1064
♢ 82
♣ AQ96

Partner opens 1♢ and naturally enough you bid 1♠. When your partner rebids 2♣ you face your first problem. You are far too strong to raise 2♣ to 3♣ as this is not forcing and you would probably feel a little uncomfortable jumping to 4♣, as this bypasses 3NT which could easily be the best game. On the other side of the coin, an immediate jump to 3NT suffers from the obvious flaw of having nothing resembling a stopper in the unbid suit.

Thirty years ago this hand would have posed a genuine problem but these days most players have adopted a convention known as Fourth Suit Forcing, whereby a bid of the fourth suit (in our example 2♡) need not show any particular holding in the suit. It simply maintains fluidity in the sequence and forces partner to make another bid to try and describe his hand. So, in our example, you can elect to bid 2♡ and listen to what partner has to say.

In practice, over 2♡, opener bids 2♠. Now what?

Given that an immediate raise of 2♣ to 3♣ would have been non forcing, most players have adopted the style that, if they use Fourth Suit Forcing (FSF) and then support openers second suit, it is forcing and that would be a convenient method for us to use here. So you bid 3♣, giving partner yet another opportunity to describe his hand, and he obliges with 3NT. Now you have to decide what to do.

Just to remind you, so far the bidding has been:

Partner	You
1♦	1♠
2♣	2♡ (FSF)
2♠	3♣
3NT	?

First of all, what is partner's shape? It is a strange sequence for partner has bid both minors, then he has supported spades and then showed something in hearts by bidding 3NT. After opening 1♦ and rebidding 2♣, we must surely expect him to hold five diamonds and four clubs which leaves only four cards in the majors. Over our 2♡ bid, he did bid 2♠, but this need not promise three cards in that suit. The truth is that with 6-4 in the minors he would have bid 3♦ and with 5-5 or more he would have bid 3♣; and with a good holding in hearts he would have bid either 2NT with a minimum or jumped to 3NT with some extra values. So, he had little alternative but to bid 2♠ with any 2-2-5-4 shape without very good hearts. When he bid 3NT over 3♣ he merely confirmed that he did hold a 2-2-5-4 shape but with something approaching a stopper in hearts – he might have as little as Qx in hearts.

How strong is he? Well, his 2♣ rebid suggested that he was not in the maximum range for a one-opening and neither his 2♠ bid nor his 3NT bid suggested that he had anything more than a minimum opener. Just for example he might have either:

	(a)	♠ Q6	*or*	(b)	♠ Q6
		♡ Q5			♡ A5
		♦ AK753			♦ KQ753
		♣ K1042			♣ K1042

even though I would personally feel more comfortable bidding 3♡ rather than 3NT holding the second example hand.

How will we fare in 3NT? In both cases the answer must be 'very badly'. If partner does have hand (a) we probably have nine top tricks but unless we are lucky the opponents will take five heart tricks before we start. If partner has hand (b) we do have a definite heart trick but we can only cash eight tricks without knocking out the ◇A. Whereupon the defence should have enough heart winners to beat the contract.

So, what is to be done? Does any other game contract look attractive?

Yes, given reasonable breaks we should be able to make eleven tricks in clubs facing either hand (a) or hand (b). We should lose just two hearts if partner has hand (a) and one heart and one diamond if he holds hand (b). So, the solution to our problem is not to pass 3NT but to bid 5♣.

It is all very easy when you come to think of it – the introduction of Fourth Suit Forcing gave us the time to let partner describe his hand and, having done so, you could almost picture his cards which allowed you to select a sensible final contract. However, to coin a common phrase – the operation was a success but the patient died, for my partner produced the following startling collection:

♠ QJ6
♡ J53
♢ AKQJ
♣ KJ10

and, needless to say, against 5♣, our opponents happily cashed three hearts.

So, why did my partner make that horrible 2♣ bid? Well, like many players he knew that he could have rebid 2NT to show a balanced hand of about this strength but he didn't like to suggest playing in no trumps with such weak hearts.

Having bid 2♣ he then had to decide what to do over 2♡. Had he jumped to 3♠ to show three card support and extra values I would have expected a 3-1-5-4 shape, so he closed his eyes and hoped that I would bid again over 2♠. He had not reckoned with my 'picturing' his hand so precisely.

That all very neatly brings us to my first rule of bidding which is simply:

'If you hold a balanced hand, bid it like a balanced hand.'

4-3-3-3, 4-4-3-2 and 5-3-3-2 distributions account for approximately 48% of the total number of hands – if we can establish a straightforward method for dealing with all of these hands, then when opener starts bidding round the houses, as in the quoted example, we should know that he possesses an unbalanced hand.

So, when we open the bidding, how should we plan to bid a balanced hand? Very simply, if the hand falls into our 1NT opening range then we should open 1NT with the possible exception of when we hold a rebiddable five card major. If we hold a hand outside our 1NT opening range and not sufficiently strong to open 2NT, then we should open one of a suit and rebid in no trumps at the appropriate level unless partner bids a suit which we can sensibly support.

There are no other possibilities!

Theorists may complain that, even playing a weak no trump, it is still considered normal to open 1♣ on a minimum strength opener with four clubs and four spades. After all, they will say if partner responds in either red suit you can sensibly rebid 1♠. However, for the structure of bidding to be easy to follow, it is much better to know that if opener bids two suits he has a distributional hand – normally he will have five cards in the first suit bid and four cards in the second with the rare exception that he might have a 4-4-4-1 distribution. So, playing the weak no trump, it would be silly to consider opening anything other than 1NT holding a hand like:

> ♠ J762
> ♡ K5
> ◇ AJ6
> ♣ KJ74

In truth, I will admit that there are some minimum openers with just 4-4 in the black suits which I would open 1♣, such as

> ♠ KJ104
> ♡ 75
> ◇ 1082
> ♣ AKQ4

but when I have bid 1♣ followed by 1♠ I will expect my partner to bid his hand on the *assumption* that I have five clubs and four spades.

I will always remember a hand that occurred in a major pairs tournament in France when I was playing with a young English international for the first time. I held:

> ♠ 75
> ♡ 4
> ◇ J108765
> ♣ A1042

My partner opened 1♣, I responded 1◇ and he bid 1♠. I gave preference to 2♣ and he bid 2NT which, given the limited nature of my bidding, must show in the region of eighteen points. What to do now? It seemed to me at the time that, weak though my hand was, it was very suitable to play in clubs; indeed if partner held prime cards such as:

> ♠ AK42
> ♡ AQ
> ◇ 42
> ♣ KQ876

even 5♣ might be possible. Of course, he was not certain to hold such excellent cards so I decided to leave him a way out by jumping to 4♣. He passed – that was no surprise – but two down was something of a rude awakening. His hand was:

♠ AQ42
♡ AK5
◇ K4
♣ Q863

Had he opened 1♠, I would either have passed or bid 1NT. After 1♠-1NT the bidding would surely have progressed 2NT-3◇-Pass; a most sensible and successful contract.

Now, if two good players can generate such a mess by introducing two suits when they have a strong balanced hand, how much more important is it that the average club player expunges this dire habit from his vocabulary.

Regardless of the strength of your 1NT opener it should not be too difficult to produce an opening bid and rebid structure to cover all balanced hands.

BALANCED HANDS:
OPENING BID AND REBID STRUCTURE

Basic System: Acol Four Card Majors: Weak No Trump (12-14)

Strength	Action
less than 12	Pass.
12-14	1NT. Exception: when you hold a rebiddable five card major you open the major.
15-17	Open one of a suit planning to rebid no trumps at minimum level. If partner bids your second suit you may raise to an appropriate level.

With two four card suits:

With both minors open 1 ◇.

With both majors open 1 ♡ (and raise a 1 ♠ response to 3 ♠).

With a major and a minor – open the major.

18-a bad 20	Open one of a suit and jump in no trumps.
A good 20-22	Open 2NT.
23-24	Open 2 ♣ and rebid in no trumps at minimum level.

BALANCED HANDS:
OPENING BID AND REBID STRUCTURE

Basic System: Acol Four Card Majors: Strong No Trump (15-17)

Strength	Action
less than 12	Pass.
12-14	Open one of a suit planning to rebid no trumps at minimum level. If partner bids your second suit you may raise to an appropriate level.

With two four card suits:

With both minors open 1 ◇

With both majors open 1 ♡ (and raise a 1 ♠ response to 2 ♠).

With a major and a minor – open the major.

Strength	Action
15-17	Open 1NT.
18- a bad 20	Open one of a suit and jump in no trumps.
A good 20-22	Open 2NT.
23-24	Open 2 ♣ and rebid in no trumps at minimum level.

Notes:

(i)   A number of players might regard 16-18 as their chosen range for a strong no trump opening. This is highly inefficient as it results in a minimum no trump rebid covering a very wide range (i.e. 12-15) and a jump rebid catering for just a nineteen point hand.

(ii) A number of leading tournament players have started playing a 14-16 1NT opening. In our approach this does have advantages with the weaker (more frequent) hands. For example, when partner responds at the two level it narrows the band of the 2NT rebid to just 12-13, which does make it easier for responder to guess what to do. The downside is that opener will be forced to jump to 3NT on a fairly wide range of 17-19 points.

OPENER'S QUIZ

Suppose that it is Love All and you are the dealer, what would you bid with each of the following hands? If you normally play a weak no trump showing 12-14 points consider the hands in the left-hand column. If you prefer to play a strong no trump showing 15-17 points then look at the hands on the right.

Before going any further, a special request. Don't just skip to the page with all the answers on it, pick up a pen and a piece of paper and write down your answer to each question. The simple truth is that the best way of learning is to benefit from your own mistakes, so make sure you put yourself to the test before reading the answers. After all, there is no point in cheating yourself.

	For Weak No Trumpers	**For Strong No Trumpers**
1.	♠ AK106 ♡ AKQ5 ◇ J72 ♣ 64	♠ AQ106 ♡ AK53 ◇ J72 ♣ 64
2.	♠ K42 ♡ J8742 ◇ KJ2 ♣ A5	♠ AQ2 ♡ J8742 ◇ K102 ♣ AQ
3.	♠ KQ43 ♡ Q6 ◇ AJ52 ♣ KJ3	♠ KQ43 ♡ Q6 ◇ AJ52 ♣ J32
4.	♠ Q1072 ♡ K2 ◇ Q53 ♣ AK42	♠ Q1072 ♡ K2 ◇ K53 ♣ AK42

	For Weak No trumpers	**For Strong No trumpers**
5.	♠ Q5 ♡ J5 ◇ KQ42 ♣ AJ742	♠ K5 ♡ Q5 ◇ KQ42 ♣ AJ742
6.	♠ AQ752 ♡ A1064 ◇ 965 ♣ 5	♠ AQ752 ♡ A1064 ◇ 965 ♣ 5
7.	♠ A1064 ♡ AQ752 ◇ 965 ♣ 5	♠ A1064 ♡ AQ752 ◇ 965 ♣ 5
8.	♠ A42 ♡ AQ9652 ◇ 75 ♣ 64	♠ A42 ♡ AQ9652 ◇ 75 ♣ 64
9.	♠ A742 ♡ KJ64 ◇ AJ74 ♣ 2	♠ AJ74 ♡ KJ64 ◇ AQ74 ♣ 2
10.	♠ AQ104 ♡ 10764 ◇ AQ74 ♣ 2	♠ AQ104 ♡ 10764 ◇ AQ74 ♣ 2

ANSWERS TO OPENER'S QUIZ

1. **(a)** Playing the weak no trump,
what do you open with:

♠ AK106
♥ AKQ5
♦ J72
♣ 64

Recommended bid: 1♥

(b) Playing the strong no trump,
what do you open with:

♠ AQ106
♥ AK53
♦ J72
♣ 64

Recommended bid: 1♥

With two good four card majors, it is tempting to open 1♠ intending to bid 2♥ on the next round. However, if you choose that route, partner will think that you have five spades and four hearts and you might find yourself given preference to a 4-2 fit. The solution is to bid 1♥ and rebid in no trumps at minimum level unless partner bids spades. If partner has a good hand with say five clubs and four spades he will respond 2♣; but you should still not miss your spade fit, as after you bid 2NT he should introduce spades at the three level. If partner turns out to be too weak to bid again after your 2NT rebid, he should not have responded 2♣, preferring to respond 1♠ instead.

2. **(a)** Playing the weak no trump,
what do you open with:

♠ K42
♥ J8742
♦ KJ2
♣ A5

Recommended bid: 1NT

(b) Playing the strong no trump,
what do you open with:

♠ AQ2
♥ J8742
♦ K102
♣ AQ

Recommended bid: 1NT

Yes, I understand that it is tempting to open your five card major, but before you open the bidding you should always consider what you are going to bid on the second round. Over 1♥ – 2♣ you are really stuck for a rebid: you can bid 2♥ but don't be surprised if partner leaves you there with a singleton. The sensible approach is to disregard poor five card suits, treat them as if there were only four cards in the suit, and open 1NT.

3. **(a)** Playing the weak no trump,   **(b)** Playing the strong no trump,
what do you open with: what do you open with:

    ♠ KQ43   ♠ KQ43
    ♡ Q6   ♡ Q6
    ◇ AJ52   ◇ AJ52
    ♣ KJ3   ♣ J32

   Recommended bid: 1♠   **Recommended bid: 1♠**

There is a view that with 4-4-3-2 hands with two non-touching suits outside the 1NT opening range, it is right to open the suit below the doubleton. The idea is that, when responder bids the two card suit, opener bids his second suit and, if responder bids the three card suit, opener can support him. The thought of opening 1◇ and calmly raising 2♣ to 3♣ fills me with dismay.

For those that play the weak no trump, it is much better to say, 'I have a balanced hand of 15-17 points with at least four spades', while opening 1♠ and rebidding 2NT showing a balanced 12-14 with a four card spade suit is a much better description if you play a strong no trump. On a good day, opening the major rather than the minor also leaves open the possibility of finding the 4-3 major fit when 3NT is wrong.

A number of players would choose to open this hand with a 'prepared' 1♣, so that they could have a comfortable rebid at the one level. Playing the strong no trump, there is some case to open with a prepared club on hands like these, indeed, without the proviso that a 2NT rebid should be 12-14 after responder introduces a new suit at the two level, it would be essential to open this hand 1♣. However, if you do adopt the prepared club style, you still have to decide whether to rebid 1NT to show the 12-14 points with or without four spades or to bid 1♠ to show at least four spades and at least three clubs!

How much more comfortable it is to play naturally: if responder is expected to have at least ten points to bid a new suit at the two level, then you can open 1♠ on hands like this and comfortably rebid 2NT over a response in a new suit at the two level.

4. **(a)** Playing the weak no trump, what do you open with:

    ♠ Q1072
    ♡ K2
    ◊ Q53
    ♣ AK42

Recommended bid: 1NT

(b) Playing the strong no trump, what do you open with:

    ♠ Q1072
    ♡ K2
    ◊ K53
    ♣ AK42

Recommended bid: 1NT

You have a balanced hand that falls within your 1NT opening range, and there is no good reason not to open 1NT, especially as your high card strength is well scattered. If you pack all your high cards into your two suits, with the clubs being better than the spades, I would have some sympathy with you treating the hand as a club/spade two suiter. However, you should remember that if you voluntarily bid two suits, your partner will expect you to have at least five cards in your first suit and four cards in the second, and he should bid accordingly.

So, weak no-trumpers might open 1♣ planning to rebid 1♠ with:

    ♠ AQ65
    ♡ 65
    ◊ 765
    ♣ AQJ5

rather than opening 1NT while strong no trump players might do the same with:

    ♠ AQJ5
    ♡ 65
    ◊ 765
    ♣ AKJ5

However, you should remember that when partner puts you back into clubs with very marginal support, he was expecting you to have five of them.

5. **(a)** Playing the weak no trump, what do you open with:

    ♠ Q5
    ♡ J5
    ◊ KQ42
    ♣ AJ742

Recommended bid: 1NT

(b) Playing the strong no trump, what do you open with:

    ♠ K5
    ♡ Q5
    ◊ KQ42
    ♣ AJ742

Recommended bid: 1NT

Here once again you have a hand that falls into the range of your 1NT opening, but a 5-4-2-2 distribution is not normally regarded as balanced so what are the alternatives? There are two – you could open with either 1♣ or 1♢, but before choosing either you should consider what you are going to do on the next round.

If you open 1♢ and partner responds in a major you are really forced into bidding your club suit. Nothing wrong with that, you might think, except that partner will think that you have at least five diamonds and four clubs and, when he gives you preference to diamonds and puts two cards in both minors down in the dummy, you are likely to be at least marginally disappointed.

Alternatively, what is going to happen if you open 1♣ and partner responds in a major? You face an interesting choice of evils. You can either repeat your poor quality club suit when partner should expect less high card strength but a better suit or you can overbid by reversing into 2♢. If you choose the latter remember that most partners would expect this bid to show in the region of seventeen points, so they will drive to game with a respectable eight count and, this time, it will be their turn to be disappointed with the dummy.

In any system there are always hands that don't fit well into any compartment. Clearly any particular choice might work out well on any particular hand and you have to make a choice between less than perfect alternatives. Here the potential flaws in choosing to open either 1♣ or 1♢ make 1NT by far the most attractive choice. Admittedly partner will not expect you to have a doubleton in *both* majors but certainly he will not be at all surprised at you having a doubleton in *either* one.

6. (a) Playing the weak no trump, what do you open with:

♠ AQ752
♡ A1064
♢ 965
♣ 5

Recommended bid: 1♠

(b) Playing the strong no trump, what do you open with:

♠ AQ752
♡ A1064
♢ 965
♣ 5

Recommended bid: 1♠

Yes, I know that you only have ten high card points but this hand qualifies as a minimum opening bid. Indeed, it even qualifies under the 'Rule of 19' as it has ten high card points and nine cards in the two longest suits. Two aces provide the expected defensive strength and 5-4-3-1 shapes always tend to play well. Add to that the fact that you have both majors and can describe your hand quite well, by opening 1♠ and rebidding 2♡ with the expected 5-4 distribution.

On the minus side, it is possible that partner will drive too high with no fit for either of your suits or if he has too many 'wasted' values facing your singleton club; but against that you are likely to reach a thin game when you do have a fit and you are particularly well placed in any part-score battle. So open 1♠.

7. **(a)** Playing the weak no trump, what do you open with:

♠ A1064
♡ AQ752
◇ 965
♣ 5

Recommended bid: Pass

(b) Playing the strong no trump, what do you open with:

♠ A1064
♡ AQ752
◇ 965
♣ 5

Recommended bid: Pass

Curiously enough this hand also qualifies as an opening bid under the 'Rule of 19': it has the same 5-4-3-1 distribution, the same pointage and the same two aces and both majors, but I would not recommend opening the bidding. Why not? Well, if you do open the bidding, you have no convenient way of describing your hand. If you opened 1♡ and partner responded 1♠ you would be delighted to support him, but if he responded 2♣ you would be forced to rebid your heart suit which gives a rather poor description of the hand. Using two bids to describe nine of your cards is much more illuminating than using two bids just to convey the fact that you have a five card suit – especially so when on many occasions your partner should expect you to have a six card suit to bid this way.

As a general rule, if you are the dealer, it is not worth opening light on any hand unless you can describe it well. If you happen to play a mini no trump opening then fair enough, but if you play the weak no trump then you should have something approximating to 12-14 balanced points when you open 1NT. Of course, there is room to upgrade a good-looking eleven point hand to twelve but opening any old eleven point hand figures to be a losing policy in the long run. After all, your partner should bid as if you have guaranteed twelve points and therefore you will get too high on many occasions.

With distributional hands it is much the same story. If you know you can describe your hand well on the first two rounds of the bidding then it is worth considering opening light, but otherwise don't bother. One final word of caution: be particularly wary of 4-4-4-1 shaped hands as experience suggests that unlike 5-4-3-1 shapes they don't play well *and* they always tend to be good in defence when the opponents play the hand, as most of the time their suits will not break well.

8. **(a)** Playing the weak no trump, what do you open with:

    ♠ A42
    ♡ AQ9652
    ◊ 75
    ♣ 64

Recommended bid: 1♡

(b) Playing the strong no trump, what do you open with:

    ♠ A42
    ♡ AQ9652
    ◊ 75
    ♣ 64

Recommended bid: 1♡

After all that, here is another first in hand, routine opener. Once again this hand qualifies as an opening bid under the 'Rule of 19' and we have no trouble describing this hand as we would plan to bid and rebid hearts. In fact, in terms of playing strength this hand is the broad equivalent of a hand with thirteen high card points and five hearts – and most of you would open that! More specifically consider the power of the sixth heart. Providing you play in hearts, or perhaps even in no trumps, you will expect to take one more trick with a six card suit than a five card suit. The pack comprises forty high card points and there are thirteen tricks, so on average for each three points you should take a trick. It's obvious really, so providing you can make use of the sixth heart, it can be assigned a value of three points.

9. **(a)** Playing the weak no trump, what do you open with:

    ♠ A742
    ♡ KJ64
    ◊ AJ74
    ♣ 2

Recommended bid: 1♡

(b) Playing the strong no trump, what do you open with:

    ♠ AJ74
    ♡ KJ64
    ◊ AQ74
    ♣ 2

Recommended bid: 1♡

We finally arrive at the scourge of our system. In general terms 4-4-4-1 hands do not qualify as balanced, so we cannot sensibly open with 1NT even if they are of the right strength, though occasionally we might be able to rebid in no trumps if partner responds in our singleton. They create a problem not only because without a five card suit they are poor in playing strength but also because they are very difficult for us to describe.

After all, if we open in one suit and then rebid in another, partner expects us to have five cards in the first suit and four in the second – so in effect anything we do becomes a lie.

Until the early 1960s, all 4-4-4-1 hands tended to be opened with the suit below the singleton; however, at about that time, it was suggested that the particular distribution that we have here could be more sensibly opened with 1♡. The reason was simply that if you open 1♡ you can support spades if partner bids them and rebid 2◇ if partner happens to respond 2♣ – so with this particular 4-4-4-1 hand the normal opening bid is certainly 1♡. At least, if you follow this style religiously you can be assured that, if partner opens 1♠ and rebids in any other suit, then he must have five spades for there is no 4-4-4-1 type hand on which he would open 1♠.

This point of view became so popular that many players will tend to open a 1-4-4-4 hand with 1◇ following exactly the same principles. However I would argue that, if the hearts are good, you should open 1♡ and not 1◇ –– after all there is a large family of hands where 4♡ on a 4-3 fit may prove to be the only making game and if you don't bid them straightaway you will never get to play in that strain.

Overall, the best advice I can give is:

(1) Remember that whatever you open you must make sure you have a reasonable rebid when partner responds in your short suit.

(2) Then choose the suits that best describe your hand.

For example, consider the next example hand:

10. (a) Playing the weak no trump, what do you open with:

♠ AQ104
♡ 10764
◇ AQ74
♣ 2

Recommended bid: 1♠

(b) Playing the strong no trump, what do you open with:

♠ AQ104
♡ 10764
◇ AKQ7
♣ 2

Recommended bid: 1♠

These examples are obvious constructions to illustrate the principle. Opening this hand 1♡ planning to rebid 2◇ over a 2♣ response is tantamount to committing suicide. Remember that partner's actions will be strongly influenced by his expectation that you hold five cards in the first suit that you bid. Inviting preference on a doubleton when you hold four to the ten is no thing of beauty, and even jump support on king to three might be embarrassing.

With this type of hand you need to back your eyesight with good commonsense. Don't open 1♡, open 1♠, planning to rebid 2◊. Sure, you will still have one spade less than your partner will expect but at least, if he supports spades, it is likely to be a playable spot.

Alter the hand to something like:

♠ A654
♡ Q654
◊ AKJ5
♣ 5

and I would solve the problem by opening 1◊. If partner responds at the one level I clearly have no problem, and if he inconveniently chooses to bid 2♣ I will rebid 2NT.

Admittedly, if I am playing the weak no trump, I am a point short but, as I suggested before, there are many hands that don't conform exactly to anything and then you have to use your commonsense. In this case, by opening 1◊ you avoid all the pitfalls associated with suggesting that you hold a five card major, and give a good indication of what you would like your partner to lead should you end up defending the contract. So, I ask you: 'Is owing your partner a point such a high price to pay?'

2

THE FIRST RESPONSE

Let's start by asking you what you would bid on both of the following hands in response to a 1♣ opening from your partner:

<table>
<tr><td>(a)</td><td>♠ 75</td><td>(b)</td><td>♠ A5</td></tr>
<tr><td></td><td>♡ KQ75</td><td></td><td>♡ KQ75</td></tr>
<tr><td></td><td>◊ Q854</td><td></td><td>◊ Q854</td></tr>
<tr><td></td><td>♣ 1042</td><td></td><td>♣ K102</td></tr>
</table>

The popular view of responding with two four card suits is that you should bid your lowest one, so on both of these hands I would expect the majority of players to bid 1◊. The theoretical argument for bidding this way is simply that, by responding in our lowest suit, it gives us the maximum chance of finding a 4-4 fit in either of our suits. If he has four hearts we would expect partner to rebid 1♡ and if he has four diamonds he should support us straightaway.

Certainly it is true that, if opener has a weak hand with five clubs and four diamonds, we might miss our diamond fit by responding 1♡, though it is also true to say that, if partner has a good enough hand for us to make a game contract in diamonds facing hand (a), then he will be strong enough himself to reverse into 2◊ on the next round. Accordingly, you may not be totally surprised to hear that I believe that 1♡ is the right response in both cases! Let's look at each hand in turn.

Hand (a)

Notice straightaway that, while we have more than sufficient to make a response to 1♣, our expectation is that, unless partner shows substantial extra values, we are only going to make minimal noises on this hand. Whichever red suit we bid, if partner rebids 1♠ we are going to bid 1NT or give preference to 2♣, and if partner rebids 1NT or 2♣ we are going to pass. So first of all we should be planning to make just one voluntary bid and 1♡ gives a much better description of where our assets are than 1◊. In the long term, your partner will have a much better chance of judging what to do if you show him the assets you have rather than those you haven't.

There are a number of reasons for this:

1. If you respond 1◇ and find partner with three diamonds and a singleton heart in a strong distributional hand, he is likely to find your actual holdings most disappointing when he comes to rest in a high level club contract but, if he holds three hearts and a singleton diamond and you bid 1♡, he certainly won't be disappointed.

2. If the opponents enter the auction and partner decides to support you on a marginal hand, you will be much better off playing in your best suit rather than your worst one.

3. Let's suppose that you do have a 4-4 heart fit and you respond 1◇ only to hear the next hand bid 1♠ or worse still 2♠, are you still so confident that you are going to find your major suit fit?

4. Then suppose that your opponents actually have the effrontery to play the hand and your partner is on lead, is he supposed to find a heart lead when you have responded 1◇?

No, however I look at it, it is much better to bid a suit where you have values than one where you haven't. However, that is not the only reason for responding 1♡ on this type of hand. Let's suppose that partner has a hand something like:

♠ 94
♡ A93
◇ AK6
♣ AQJ65

Now, where would you like to play this hand facing your motley collection, which if you remember is:

♠ 75
♡ KQ75
◇ Q854
♣ 1042

Yes, I think you've twigged. The best game contract is undoubtedly 4♡! – a contract that is unlikely to be on the menu if you respond 1◇ but which you might just reach if you bid 1♡. Whichever red suit you respond in, your partner is likely to rebid 2NT – showing a balanced 18-19, so you have the values to go on and with good hearts and three card club support a careful bidder might just continue with 3◇. Opener should now show his three card heart support and with only a small doubleton in spades you should really try a fourth suit 3♠, to try and see what partner chooses to do. Clearly, with no semblance of a spade stopper, he will want to play in either clubs or hearts.

Now, I'm not pretending that such a sequence would be easy for most pairs to produce at the table, but if you don't respond 1♡ you have absolutely no chance of hitting the jackpot. Remember that with most balanced hands without a primary fit the most likely game destination is 3NT, but on many hands a good 4-3 fit in a major may be a sensible alternative. So, apart from the maxim of bidding good suits before bad ones, also try to respond in a decent four card major suit rather than bidding a four card diamond suit.

Hand (b)

Quite clearly, our second example is a totally different kettle of fish. Partner has opened the bidding with 1♣ and you are looking at:

♠ A5
♡ KQ75
◇ Q854
♣ K102

First of all, facing even the most minimum opening bid, we must plan to be in game, but which one? The most likely destinations are 4♡, 5♣ and 3NT – so, to describe our hand well, we need to show our heart suit and show a game going hand with clubs at a low enough level to play in 3NT. The best start to this plan must be to bid our good major suit.

Furthermore, just as in our previous example, it will be difficult to get out of no trumps to either a 4-3 heart fit or to a 5-3 club fit when it is right, if we start by responding 1◇.

Let's consider what you would bid on the next round if partner rebids 1♠. First, if you have chosen to respond 1◇ on the first round, you have a game going hand with very good hearts, so the normal bid would seem to be 3NT. Alternatively, if you start with 1♡ you have a much better choice on the next round. Admittedly, many players would still blast into 3NT but those with a good understanding of Fourth Suit Forcing are likely to proceed with 2◇.

Note that if partner holds something like...

♠ K987
♡ A92
◇ 7
♣ AQJ96

after the following bidding sequence:

1♣	1◇
1♠	3NT
?	

he would have little option but to pass, but after:

1♣	1♡
1♠	2◇
?	

he has a comfortable jump to 3♡ available, and with opener painting a picture of a reasonable 4-3-1-5 hand it should not be impossible for you to recognise the considerable potential of the combined hands (note just how important it is to know that after 1♣–1♡–1♠ partner does have five clubs and four spades).The full sequence might be:

1♣	1♡
1♠	2◇
3♡	4♣
4NT	5◇
6♣	Pass

Despite a combined holding of only twenty-eight high card points, the hands fit particularly well so that 6♣ is an excellent contract. By contrast note that when opener has a subsidiary fit for your diamond suit such as in:

♠ K987
♡ 6
◇ A92
♣ AQJ96

then 6♣ is a terrible contract and 3NT, which we will reach regardless of whether we respond 1◇ or 1♡, is right.

Of course, there is a moral to the story: in response, don't start your campaign by bidding a bad four card suit when you have a good hand!

Responding to 1NT

So far, I have said nothing about an area of the game which many pairs devote a lot of time to developing, that is responding to 1NT. I am not going to say too much on this particular subject and far be it from me to try and stop players devoting many hours of their valuable time to honing up on their sophisticated methods. However, I firmly believe that, in practice, all this wonderful machinery makes little contribution to improving their results at the table. Indeed, while Stayman in some form or other would be fairly high on my list of essential conventional aids, I have to say that transfers in any one of their many guises would have very low priority. I have no intention of wasting too much space reploughing regularly tilled soil; however, whatever methods you employ there are some hand types which seem to be notoriously difficult to handle well. Let's consider an example:

♠ AQ42	♠ K105
♡ 75	♡ 84
◇ A954	◇ K82
♣ K104	♣ AQ762

With West as dealer, playing a weak no trump, he has little option but to open 1NT and who could criticise East for simply raising to 3NT. Nobody would deny that East's hand is full value for a raise to game, but barring miracles the opponents will take the first five heart tricks to beat the contract – and, what is worse, 4♠ and, for that matter, 5♣ are much better spots.

This situation is totally unsatisfactory yet it only takes a moment's consideration to find a fairly reliable way of bidding this pair of hands to the top spot. Let's suppose that East starts his campaign by using Stayman – yes, I know he doesn't actually have a four card major but bear with me for the moment. So, the auction starts:

1NT	2♣
2♠	?

What should East do now? Well, I know what I want to bid, and that is 3♣, natural, forcing to game but unsure of the final destination. Now, the whole auction should be:

1NT	2♣
2♠	3♣
3◇	3♠
4♠	Pass

With nothing in hearts, but values in both of the minors, West is careful to bid 3◊, showing where his outside values are. Again, with nothing in hearts, East takes the opportunity to show his three card support for spades, and West completes the exercise by raising to game as his spades are quite good. With poorer spades and better diamonds, West might consider bidding 4♣ as 5♣ might then be a better spot than 4♠.

Without any doubt, adopting this free-wheeling exploratory style has been worth bushels of points over the years especially in teams play, and I would thoroughly recommend it.

Obviously this would mean a total change of method if you still play that 2♣ Stayman followed by 3♣ is to play; however, you might like to consider whether the upside of being able to conduct natural exploratory auctions of the type shown in our example is more than adequate compensation for the very rare hand when passing 1NT rather than running out into 3♣ proves to be a disaster.

Relaxing the requirement that a hand that uses Stayman *must* have a four card major is also a small price to pay. After all, the inference would still be that, if responder rebids 2NT or 3NT after using Stayman, he must have at least one four card major.

For those of you who already play an involved system of transfers, please consider how you would handle this type of hand. If the honest answer is 'Probably, not very well', then consider using Stayman followed by three of either minor in this way. I firmly believe that you will find this a lot more beneficial than using a sequence like:

1NT   2♣
2♠   3♣

to show an invitational strength hand with four hearts and at least five clubs – a method that seems quite popular in some transferring circles.

QUIZ I FOR RESPONDER'S

In each case, your partner opens 1♡, what do you respond?

1.   ♠ Q8765
    ♡ AJ6
    ◇ K5
    ♣ 1042

5.   ♠ Q872
    ♡ K2
    ◇ 75
    ♣ KJ872

2.   ♠ J8765
    ♡ AJ62
    ◇ K5
    ♣ 42

6.   ♠ KJ87
    ♡ K2
    ◇ 75
    ♣ KJ872

3.   ♠ K42
    ♡ KJ6
    ◇ K1082
    ♣ A105

7.   ♠ A7
    ♡ AJ62
    ◇ 42
    ♣ KJ872

4.   ♠ K42
    ♡ K6
    ◇ K1082
    ♣ AJ105

8.   ♠ A72
    ♡ AJ62
    ◇ KJ
    ♣ J742

ANSWERS TO RESPONDER'S QUIZ I

In each case, your partner opens 1♡, what do you respond?

1.   ♠ Q8765
                                      ♡ AJ6
                                      ◇ K5
                                      ♣ 1042

Recommended bid: 1♠

We start with a relatively easy one. Even if partner has five hearts he may still have four spades, so our first move is to bid 1♠ before supporting hearts on the next round. If for example partner rebids 2◇ we are worth a limit raise to 3♡, showing three card support for partner's presumed five card suit and inviting him to press on to game with more than minimum values. Yes, when opener rebids 2◇, he should be expected to have five hearts because with a balanced hand of any strength he should have either opened in no trumps, rebid in no trumps or supported your 1♠ response.

2.   ♠ J8765
                                      ♡ AJ62
                                      ◇ K5
                                      ♣ 42

Recommended bid: 3♡

This is fairly similar to the last hand except that we are blessed with four card trump support for partner's major suit. If we introduce spades and then jump to 3♡ when partner rebids two of a minor (as we did on the last example), partner can only be certain of three card support. Therefore it is right to give him the good news straightaway by supporting hearts.

How many should we bid? In standard methods, the limit raise to 3♡ shows about 10-11 points and four card trump support. Here we only have nine high card points but we have extra distributional values. The 5-4-2-2 shape is much better than the more normal 4-4-3-2 shape: in playing the hand partner should benefit from the extra ruffing value in the minor suits or the chance of establishing the spade suit.

If I were forced to select between the two alternatives of under bidding with just a simple raise to 2♡ or over bidding with a leap to game, I would prefer the latter on the basis that there are some fairly minimum opening hands where partner might pass 3♡ only to find that the hands fit rather well and the game may be made. For example, holding:

♠ KQ
♡ K9873
◇ A742
♣ 87

partner will pass 3♡ and the game depends on little more than the hearts breaking evenly.

3.
♠ K42
♡ KJ6
◇ K1082
♣ A105

Recommended bid: 3NT

One of the most frequently misused bids in good standard Acol is the immediate response of 3NT after partner has opened with one of a major. Many players believe that this immediate 3NT response should simply mean that they wish to play in 3NT regardless – that is unless partner has sufficient values to explore a possible slam. The bid clearly shows a game-going balanced hand without the ability to bid the other major but how many cards should it promise in partner's suit – two or three?

I am a firm believer that over openings of one of a major the immediate jump responses of both 2NT and 3NT should *guarantee* three card support, and that both bids invite partner to help make the decision on what the contract should be. If he can be certain of three card support then he can judge whether to play in 3NT, remove to four of his major or, with a better hand, he can explore the slam possibilities with much greater safety knowing that he always has a safe haven in which to play.

Furthermore, if I am not allowed to respond 3NT on hands of this type, then what am I to bid? A 2◇ response to 1♡ normally shows five cards in the suit and when partner rebids his hearts I have little alternative but to raise him to game regardless. He may well be disappointed with my lack of ruffing values, but I can barely make a unilateral decision to play in 3NT after he has rebid his suit.

4.   ♠ K42
                                ♡ K6
                                ◇ K1082
                                ♣ AJ105

Recommended bid: 2♣

This is the reverse of the coin: a game going-hand, no spade suit and good cover in both minors – everybody's 3NT bid except that you do not have three card heart support. Notice that without three hearts you must hold either a five card suit or two four card suits, so what is the panic?

By bidding 2♣, we give ourselves the chance to find a fit in either minor and if partner does rebid 2♡ we can still bid 3NT on the next round.

5.   ♠ Q872
                                ♡ K2
                                ◇ 75
                                ♣ KJ872

Recommended bid: 1♠

Although you have nine points and a fair five card suit, the natural 2♣ bid risks losing a 4-4 spade fit. If opener holds five or six hearts and four spades without the strength to reverse, over 2♣ he will be endplayed into rebidding his hearts. Of course, you could continue by bidding spades yourself but this would be an overbid taking you to at least 2NT facing any minimum opener. With a hand of this shape you should always bid 1♠ unless you are strong enough to bid both of your suits in natural order.

6.   ♠ KJ87
                                ♡ K2
                                ◇ 75
                                ♣ KJ872

Recommended bid: 2♣

I have always found it strange that, now we have the strength to bid both our suits in the natural order, many players are seduced by the quality of their spades to bid them first. Curiously, starting with 1♠ on this hand is potentially much more damaging than responding 2♣ on the previous hand. On hand five you would be a little unlucky to miss 4♠ by respond-ing 2♣ but on this hand you will be in considerable difficulty if partner simply rebids his hearts. If you introduce your clubs at the three level you will be committed to playing in game, and partner will expect you to have five spades. No, if you do bid 1♠ on the first round your best continuation over a 2♡ rebid is to raise to 3♡, giving your partner the option to proceed to 4♡ with a good minimum opener. Of course, you might miss 3NT in this way but at least you will not have put your head indiscriminately on the chopping block.

How much simpler it is to bid your suits in their natural order. Respond 2♣ and if partner rebids 2♡ introduce your spades. If opener rebids 2◇ instead you have a comfortable 2NT continuation.

7.   ♠ A7
                                                ♡ AJ62
                                                ◇ 42
                                                ♣ KJ872

Recommended bid: 2♣

With a good opening bid and four card support for partner's major, it is quite clear that this hand belongs in at least game. However, rather than just raise to game, it may help partner to judge the slam prospects more clearly if we let him know that we have a reasonable club fit. By bidding 2♣ and then jumping to game in hearts if he rebids 2◇, we paint a good picture of our hand. Not quite strong enough to jump in clubs straightaway but good enough to consider a slam if the opener had some sort of fit in clubs.

For example, suppose that the opener holds:

                                                ♠ 97
                                                ♡ KQ983
                                                ◇ A987
                                                ♣ AQ

Facing a decent five card club suit and good hearts you can already 'see' eleven tricks and presumably responder must have some other cards outside clubs and hearts. In essence I would believe it right to decide to bid 6♡ provided that partner can provide a spade control. To find out I would make a cuebid of 5♣ which in itself already suggests that I am looking for a spade control. If responder bids 5◇ I would sign off on 5♡, if he just bids 5♡ I will pass but hopefully on this hand he will recognise the importance of his spade control and take the plunge to the six level.

8.

        ♠ A72
        ♡ AJ62
        ◇ KJ
        ♣ J742

Recommended bid: 4◇

This example is included because it is one of the few areas of the game where I believe some conventional aid is of particular use to the average player. If we bid 2♣ and follow it with 4♡ as we did on the previous example partner will expect better clubs and may press on for the wrong reason. Equally with a pronounced shortage in clubs he is likely to pass on the reasonable assumption that you have wasted values in clubs. For example, holding:

        ♠ KQ6
        ♡ KQ872
        ◇ A987
        ♣ 5

partner will pass, only to find that 6♡ is cold. (Notice that facing our previous hand 6♡ is terrible.)

Equally if we just raise 1♡ to 4♡ partner will not really know that we have so many high cards. After all would you not raise 1♡ to 4♡ on something like:

        ♠ 7
        ♡ AJ643
        ◇ 104
        ♣ KQ872

To cope with this problem, I would recommend that you should play some form of Swiss to help distinguish between high card and distributional raises to four of either major.

There are lots of different varieties, some of which just employ the rarely used bids of 4♣ and 4◇ as immediate responses to one of a major and some that use all the double jump bids in a new suit after the one of a major opening. For example, if you chose to jump to 3♠ to show a spade control plus good trump support you were already using a simple version of Swiss – and you had better have agreed this with your partner or else you might find yourself playing in spades!

For simplicity, I am going to recommend a variety of Swiss known as Fruit Machine.

The immediate response of 4♣ shows a high card raise to four of the major with one of three possibilities:

- **(a)** Three aces.
- **(b)** Two aces and the king of trumps.
- **(c)** Two aces and a side-suit singleton.

If your partner needs to know which, he can proceed with a relay of 4◇ asking and then with:

- **(a)** Three aces, you bid 4NT
- **(b)** Two aces and the king of trumps, you bid four of the trump suit.
- **(c)** Two aces and a side suit singleton, you bid your short suit.

The immediate jump to 4◇ shows a high-card raise to four of the major without the requirements to bid 4♣. This type of hand is sometimes beautifully described as a 'pudding raise'. In fact, our example eight would be a good example of a pudding raise.

For players whose slam bidding is inexorably based on the use of Gerber, the sacrifice of the 4♣ bid to the virtues of Swiss may just be too much to bear. However, at the very least it does make sense to adopt the 4◇ bid as a pudding raise – at least the hands with good controls that fit into the 4♣ (Fruit Machine) Swiss bids are more easily described in other ways than the more ordinary balanced high card raises to game.

For those who want to play an even more modern Swiss variation, the idea of using splinters might appeal. The idea is that an unnecessary jump in a new suit agrees partners suit and shows a shortage in the suit bid. So, for example, after a 1♡ opening you might bid an immediate 4♣ holding:

♠ A654
♡ AQ65
◇ Q1043
♣ 8

Clearly, this method is particularly good in helping partner to make an assessment of whether his hand is 'working' or not. For example, with:

♠ Q82
♡ KJ1087
◇ A6
♣ KQ6

opener does have more than a minimum opening bid, but slam prospects are poor as he only has ten points outside clubs and no particularly good distribution. He should sign off in 4♡.

Contrast this, with:

♠ KQ2
♡ KJ1087
◇ A6
♣ 653

However you look at it, this is a minimum opening hand, yet with no wasted values in clubs a heart slam is in the offing. Facing our example splinter hand you would still need some good fortune to make twelve tricks, but add the ♠J to either hand, or replace the ◇Q with the ◇K and the slam would be excellent. So clearly this opening hand should make a more encouraging bid than 4♡, the obvious choice being a cuebid of 4◇.

If you decide to play splinters the good news is that it is a method that is easily adaptable to other situations. For example, after:

1♠   2♡
?

bids of 4♣ and 4◇ can be used as splinters, showing a good heart raise with shortage in the suit bid. Similarly, after:

1♠   2♣
2♡   ?

a bid of 4◇ could be a splinter showing shortage in diamonds and four card heart support.

Of course, the bad news is that you still won't have solved the problem of what to do with a balanced raise to game with four card support. Some players have solved this problem by giving up the natural 3NT response and using 3NT to show a balanced high card raise to game. While this is probably the easiest option, there are some much more complicated arrangements available. For example, it is not difficult to devise a scheme whereby the lowest splinter bid, i.e. 3♠ over 1♡ or 4♣ over 1♠, is either a splinter or a balanced raise to game, with opener using the next step up as a relay to find out.

Whichever method you choose, I strongly recommend that you adopt some conventional aid to distinguish between high card and distributional raises to four of a major.

RESPONDER'S QUIZ II

Your partner opens 1♠. What do you respond holding:

1. ♠ K42
   ♡ KQ82
   ◇ K104
   ♣ QJ4

2. ♠ K42
   ♡ KQ842
   ◇ K10
   ♣ QJ4

3. ♠ K42
   ♡ Q762
   ◇ J76
   ♣ Q76

4. ♠ K42
   ♡ K762
   ◇ 76
   ♣ Q762

5. ♠ KQ42
   ♡ 87
   ◇ 53
   ♣ AKQ72

6. ♠ K2
   ♡ AJ2
   ◇ QJ5
   ♣ AK1072

7. ♠ K2
   ♡ K5
   ◇ AK1072
   ♣ AJ72

8. ♠ K42
   ♡ 87
   ◇ AK1072
   ♣ AK5

ANSWERS TO RESPONDER'S QUIZ II

Your partner opens 1♠, what do you respond holding:

1.   ♠ K42
                                      ♡ KQ82
                                      ◇ K104
                                      ♣ QJ4

Recommended bid: 3NT

If there was any doubt in your mind as to whether an immediate response of 3NT to an opening of one of a major should show two or three card support, this is the hand type that should resolve the issue. For an immediate response of 2♡ to 1♠ you are expected to have a five card heart suit, and certainly opener should be encouraged to support a 2♡ response with only three trumps. So with only four hearts and no other suit what are we expected to do? The only alternative to an immediate jump in no trumps is to enter the world of inventive bidding and make up a suit, the popular choice being to respond 2♣.

With a solid fourteen points opposite an opening bid we must make sure that we arrive in game so the only possible response is 3NT. Take away the ♠K and you would still have enough to bid 2NT – the same hand type but only invitational strength. Notice that with five spades and four hearts opener can comfortably remove 3NT to 4♡ – giving you the choice of games. This would not be such a successful action if you could have a 2-3-4-4 shape.

2.   ♠ K42
                                      ♡ KQ842
                                      ◇ K10
                                      ♣ QJ4

Recommended bid: 2♡

This hand was initially included in my classes as a counterbalance to the last example. With five hearts and a game-going hand of no particular distinction it is totally normal just to bid 2♡, if partner rebids 2♠ we have a comfortable raise to 4♠ and he if he rebids 2NT we raise to 3NT (probably via 3♠) regardless of whether his rebid is weak or strong.

Imagine my surprise that over 40% of players in my classes have wanted to jump to 3♡ straightaway. With no aces, a poor heart suit and only fourteen points, I can see no reason to be suggesting that we have an interest in anything higher than game unless partner has such an interest himself. To jump the bidding in a new suit the normal expectation is a sixteen point hand with a good suit or some support for opener – and this hand does not qualify. If you do bid 3♡ on the first round and partner rebids 3♠ your choices are clear. You can either continue with 4♠, hoping that partner will not go on expecting a rather better hand, or you can bid 3NT, suggesting a balanced hand in the 16-18 point region.

3.   ♠ K42
                                          ♡ Q762
                                          ◇ J76
                                          ♣ Q76

Recommended bid: 1NT

An obvious 1NT bid but 2♠ may work out well if partner has a 5-3-3-2 shape with insufficient strength to bid again over 1NT. Note that opener should bid his second suit with a 5-4 shape even if he has a very weak hand and he should rebid spades only if he has a six card suit.

4.   ♠ K42
                                          ♡ K762
                                          ◇ 76
                                          ♣ Q762

Recommended bid: 2♠

Yes, we still only have eight points just as last time, however, the doubleton diamond promises the possibility of scoring a ruff playing in a spade contract; which should swing the balance between supporting partner and bidding 1NT.

One of the greatest advantages of raising spades on a hand of this type is that is that it removes much of the pressure for partner to rebid his moth-eaten five card spade suit when we do actually respond 1NT. Occasionally his 2♠ rebid works well, especially if we have a hand like the one in this example and, unless we learn to bid 2♠ on hands like this, he will continue to bid 2♠ over 1NT regardless of the number of times he gets a bad result when you have a singleton or doubleton spade.

Certainly, over the years I have been surprised by a substantial minority who want to bid 2♣ rather than 2♠. They argue that with eight points and a partial fit for partner they are strong enough to bid at the two level. That may be so, but the choice of 2♣ reveals a lack of thought about what they intend to do on the next round.

For example, over 2◊ they propose to bid 2♠. Fair enough but preference at the two level is consistent with holding just a doubleton spade. For example, what else can you do on:

♠ 42
♡ K762
◊ 76
♣ KQJ106

Notice that if opener holds:

♠ AQ765
♡ Q5
◊ AQ532
♣ 5

he should pass the simple preference to 2♠ but make a game try after a simple raise to 2♠.

Even worse, if opener raises 2♣ to 3♣ they could be playing in a very inferior contract and even if he rebids 2NT showing a strong no trump responder will have to guess whether to drive on with 3♠ in case his partner has five spades or pass 2NT and hope that he hasn't.

Overall, it is much better to bid 2♠ straightaway; after all if you had:

♠ Q762
♡ K762
◊ 76
♣ K42

which is a better hand in support of spades, you would raise 1♠ to 2♠ without giving the matter any further consideration.

5.   ♠ KQ42
                                          ♡ 87
                                          ◊ 53
                                          ♣ AKQ72

Recommended bid: 3♣

While this hand may only be fourteen points in theory, it is worth a lot more in support of spades. Indeed 6♠ will roll facing many a minimum opener including two aces (one of which is the ♠A) and some form of control in the remaining suit. For example:

♠ A8763
♡ A942
◇ K5
♣ J4

would make the slam lay down even without a favourable diamond lead unless trumps are 4-0 or clubs are 5-1. Accordingly, it is a nonsense to believe that treating this hand as a delayed game raise by responding 2♣ and jumping to 4♠ on the next round does it justice. Jump to 3♣ and raise spades on the next round.

6.

♠ K2
♡ AJ2
◇ QJ5
♣ AK1072

Recommended bid: 3♣

Jump to 3♣, planning to rebid 3NT on the next round. The real problem with starting with a simple 2♣ bid is that you will have no sensible way of getting the hand off your chest next time round. 2♣ followed by 3NT should not conceal a hand of better than about fifteen points, for you cannot expect opener to press on with a suitable thirteen or fourteen point hand for fear of getting too high.

Any other choice defies the imagination.

7.

♠ K2
♡ K5
◇ AK1072
♣ AJ72

Recommended Bid: 2◇

I would not be at all surprised if you also jumped to 3◇ to try and get this hand off your chest but the problem with that should soon become clear. Let's suppose that partner rebids 3♠ – now what are you going to do?

Obviously you might well settle for 3NT – not a totally bad description of the hand but you have not given yourself any chance of finding a possible club fit. Alternatively if you continue with 4♣ you may come up smelling of roses but you also may be heading for the stratosphere with no real fit – and are you sure that if opener rebids 4NT you will take it as natural and not Blackwood?

No, it is for this reason that most good players have adopted the view that it is ill-advised to jump in a new suit with a two suited hand. The initial response of 2◇ is forcing and you plan to bid the clubs on the next round. You can show your general strength later after you have found out whether you have a fit or not.

8.   ♠ K42
                                         ♡ 87
                                         ◇ AK1072
                                         ♣ AK5

Recommended Bid: 3◇

This hand illustrates the reverse of the coin. If we are not going to jump in a new suit with a two suiter what can a sequence such as 1♠-3◇-3♠-4♣ possibly show?

Happily the obvious conclusion is that it must show a hand with support for partner, with the 4♣ bid being a cuebid agreeing partners spades in this case.

Overall, it is well worth noting the various types of hands on which it is sensible to make a jump response in a new suit. They are:

1. A hand such as Example 5, where you have an excellent suit of your own plus a good fit for partner where you plan to jump in your suit and then support partner.

2. A hand of 16-18 points such as Example 6 with no particular fit for partner but good cover in both the other suits. Here you plan to jump in your suit and rebid 3NT.

3. A hand of 16+ points in value with at least three card support for partner where you will jump in your best suit and then bid another suit which will be a cuebid agreeing partner's first bid suit. Hand 8 is an excellent example.

4. A hand with a very good suit of your own – normally a one loser suit or better! – where you plan to rebid your own suit setting that suit as trumps and inviting partner to cuebid.

There are no other possibilities!.

3
OPENER'S REBID

Let's start by posing a straightforward question. Suppose you deal your-self the following reasonable collection:

♠ QJ5
♡ AK65
◇ QJ872
♣ 5

You open the bidding with 1◇ and with the opposition silent your partner responds 1♠. What would your rebid be?

When I first set this question to one of my classes, I was confidently expect-ing that a large majority would bid 2◇ rather than elect for what I regard as an automatic raise to 2♠. You can only imagine my surprise when I found that about half of a class of some forty experienced players made neither of those choices, electing instead to show their second suit by 'reversing' into 2♡. Most of the remaining players had chosen to rebid their diamond suit while just two or three rather hesitantly suggested that they might support their partner.

In fact, I can safely say that it was the ensuing discussion of this particular deal that drove home to me the message that many average players really do flounder like fish in the sea. After all, this is not an issue that has any-thing whatsoever to do with learning a new system, or even a new-fangled treatment, it is simply an application of the fundamental principles of bid-ding. I was horrified, but, on reflection, it was clear that this lack of under-standing was primarily due to the fact that, despite their many years of playing the game, most of my class had never been introduced to the ideas involved.

Certainly, in this country, it is very easy to find a basic bridge class but after one short course of beginners lessons perhaps followed by a so-called 'Intermediate' course, you are left out there to fend for yourself. Sometimes, if you are lucky, you will find a friendly good player who is prepared to devote some of his invaluable time to help you improve your game, but all too often the development of your understanding of the game is left to you, trying to unravel a myriad of conflicting advice from those who are barely any better than you. All too often, this means that for every two steps forward you take one step back: for every good lesson learned a bad habit is adopted. Most of the time it is *truly* a case of the blind leading the blind.

Let me illustrate this view by continuing the story of the example hand. Amongst the class in question there was one good, experienced tournament player who had already demonstrated a high level of card play yet not only did he bid 2♡ on this hand but he was still adamantly defending his choice a full hour later. Yes, of course he recognised that 2♡ was a reverse forcing his partner to the three level to give preference back to diamonds, and, of course, he recognised that this meant that a reverse promised a good hand but somehow it would all come out in the wash when he showed his support for spades later. Far from it, for his stated intention to bid again on the next round meant that by rebidding 2♡ he had effectively committed his side to game, facing any minimum responding hand.

The very thought of voluntarily arriving in 3NT with a collection like:

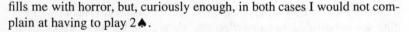

♠ K1076	**N**	♠ QJ5
♡ 972	**W E**	♡ AK65
◊ 63		◊ QJ872
♣ K964	**S**	♣ 5

or 4♠ with:

♠ K10763	**N**	♠ QJ5
♡ 972	**W E**	♡ AK65
◊ 3		◊ QJ872
♣ K964	**S**	♣ 5

fills me with horror, but, curiously enough, in both cases I would not complain at having to play 2♠.

The simple truth is that with what is essentially a minimum opening hand we should strive to:

    (a) Limit the strength of our hand as soon as possible – after all we have done our bit by opening the bidding.

    (b) Support our partner if it is at all possible.

Of course, looking at the second of these pairs of hands, it should be immediately obvious why 2♠ is a far superior rebid to 2◊. Facing a 2◊

rebid, the responding hand has little option but to pass and hope that opener manages to scramble a few tricks. Certainly he should not try to improve the contract by rebidding 2♠ lest his partner's spade support matches his own for diamonds and the 2♦ rebid could easily conceal a decent six card suit rather than the actual holding.

However, the 'obvious' reason that 2♠ figures to be a sensible contract, while 2♦ will frequently be a poor spot, is really only part of the reason why opener should support his partner on this hand.

For sake of example, let's suppose that the responder holds a much better hand, such as:

> ♠ A10763
> ♡ QJ2
> ♦ K3
> ♣ K96

then, facing a 2♦ rebid, won't he just jump to 3NT whereas after a 2♠ rebid he would at least consider 4♠?

Alternatively, suppose that the responder holds a more indeterminate hand like:

> ♠ A10763
> ♡ 94
> ♦ 104
> ♣ AJ64

Despite holding two aces most players would not consider making another bid if opener simply rebid 2♦ but after a raise to 2♠ the hand is worth a second look. Facing our example hand:

> ♠ QJ5
> ♡ AK65
> ♦ QJ872
> ♣ 5

you can see that 4♠ is certainly quite a playable contract, but to get there responder really has to know just how much the lowly ♠3 is worth!

Very simply, playing in a diamond contract responder's fifth spade is most unlikely to take a trick but playing with spades as trumps the fifth spade is almost certainly going to take a trick. It is well worth repeating that, as there are forty high card points in the pack, and thirteen tricks in a hand, on average you need about three points to make a trick. So, playing in spades, what is the value of that fifth spade? Yes, you've got it, once you know you have got a spade fit, that lowly ♠3 is worth about three points and, with twelve points facing an opening bid, even the most conservative players would at least make a game try.

Put another way, your choice of rebid is most important in helping your partner to evaluate the combined potential of the two hands and, if you want to give him a chance of making a sensible decision, you must tell him that you have already located a playable fit. In this particular case, your 3-4-5-1 shape makes this hand attractive for playing in spades. Consequently, raising 1♠ to 2♠ to show a minimum opening with diamonds and spade support gives a much better picture than just repeating your diamonds.

Average club players are frequently amazed at how often expert players seem to nose out good game contracts with little more than half the high cards in the pack. Without doubt their success is based on their ability to identify the degree of fit on each hand quickly, and it is for this reason that it is essential to support your partner whenever you have support.

Now, on a totally different theme, consider what you would do as opener with the following hand:

♠ Q94
♡ KJ543
♢ –
♣ AKQ74

There is no real problem on the first round. Your clubs might be much better than your hearts but it is much more important to get your five card major into the action rather than your five card minor, so you open 1♡. Now, suppose that your partner responds 1NT, what are you going to do next?

It is a popular misconception that just because we hold a good hand we should jump the bidding. In practice, our benchmark should be that if partner passes 2♣ will we be unhappy or, more specifically, if partner passes 2♣ are we likely to have missed a game contract?

Put in those terms, on this hand, the answer should be a categoric *no* – we will not have missed game if he passes 2♣.

First of all, which game do you have in mind? For 3NT, your partner will need a monster hand: he has to bolster the spade suit, stop the diamonds and convert your heart suit into a source of tricks. What about 4♡? Well, first, if he has three cards in hearts he will certainly strain to bid again over 2♣ even if it is only to put you back to 2♡. That leaves an outside possibility that he can fill the heart suit with a good doubleton and have sufficiently good spades – yes, that is possible but not likely. Finally, how about 5♣? Again it is most unlikely that we can make eleven tricks in clubs without partner having sufficient to raise 2♣ to 3♣. So, at worst, by bidding 2♣ we give up a very slender chance of a game contract.

Now look at 3♣. How many times will our leap drive partner into a totally unmakeable game? Quite often, I would say.

No, 2♣ is the winner and, better still, if partner bids again we get a good chance to paint an accurate picture of our hand. For example, over preference to 2♡, we can make a further try via 2♠. Knowing of your shortness in diamonds partner should downgrade cards in that suit and bid 3♡ or 4♡ accordingly.

OPENER'S REBID: QUIZ I

You open 1♡, your partner responds 1♠, what do you rebid holding:

1. ♠ A42
    ♡ AK1072
    ◇ Q102
    ♣ 54

2. ♠ A42
    ♡ AK1072
    ◇ QJ2
    ♣ A5

3. ♠ Q1042
    ♡ AKQ74
    ◇ 62
    ♣ A5

4. ♠ Q1042
    ♡ AKQ74
    ◇ 62
    ♣ AK

5. ♠ Q104
    ♡ AQJ742
    ◇ AJ3
    ♣ 2

ANSWERS TO OPENER'S REBID: QUIZ I

You open 1♡, your partner responds 1♠, what do you rebid holding:

1.   ♠ A42
                           ♡ AK1072
                           ◇ Q102
                           ♣ 54

Recommended Bid: 2♠

With a clearly rebiddable suit, both weak and strong no-trumpers open
1♡, expecting to pass a 1NT response or rebid their hearts after partner
bids two of a minor. But what if he bids 1♠? If you stop to think about it,
you have very good cards for playing in spades even if partner has only
four cards in the suit. The ♡AK figure to score whatever suit is trumps
and you have both control of the trump suit – the ♠A – and a possible
ruffing value in clubs. Of course partner might have four spades and three
hearts when 2♡ will play better than 2♠, but he may also have five
spades and only one heart, when 2♠ will play very well indeed and 2♡
may have no chance. On balance, I believe it right to support partner with
three trumps to honour and a ruffing value in a minimum opener, and
accordingly I would rebid 2♠.

Putting it another way, 1♡ followed by 2♠ suggests a minimum opener
with hearts and some spade support. 1♡ followed by 2♡ suggests a minimum opener with no spade support. Which is the more definitive description
of our hand?

Playing a strong no trump there is a further option – you could bid 1NT to
show your balanced minimum without support for spades. However, the
prime nature of your cards still suggests that a 2♠ bid would be more
descriptive. After all, if partner has as little as:

                           ♠ KQ876
                           ♡ 84
                           ◇ KJ85
                           ♣ 87

game in spades would be a fair proposition, but playing in hearts or no
trumps you would be lucky to make more than eight tricks.

2.   ♠ A42
                                          ♡ AK1072
                                          ◇ QJ2
                                          ♣ A5

Recommended Bid: 2NT

Most players seem to be on the right wavelength here – the 2NT rebid should show a balanced hand of 18-19 points which may include either five hearts or three spades or both. Responder can still check back to look for an eight card major fit.

Almost inevitably, there will be some players who will look elsewhere. The hand is quite good in terms of its support for spades, but a jump to 3♠ is reserved for hands with four card support that are not worth raising 1♠ to game, while a jump rebid in hearts shows a slightly weaker hand in terms of overall high card strength but with a good six card heart suit. Meanwhile, some of those who might be called the more scientific bidders are heading for trouble in another way: 2◇ could easily become the final contract with either 4♠ or 3NT makeable while the immediate jump to 3◇ is categorically game forcing facing any heap of rhubarb. There are times when it can be sensible to invent a suit to bid but not when there is a fully descriptive bid available.

3.   ♠ Q1042
                                          ♡ AKQ74
                                          ◇ 62
                                          ♣ A5

Recommended Bid: 3♠

With four card support and substantially better than a minimum opening, it is right to make the invitational limit raise to 3♠. In case of doubt, I would much prefer to take a shot at 4♠ than languish in 2♠.

4.   ♠ Q1042
                                          ♡ AKQ74
                                          ◇ 62
                                          ♣ AK

Recommended Bid: 4♣

Putting this example to my classes has always produced a very wide range of opinion but at least the majority have recognised that the hand belongs

in game in spades. Quite a few players have always wanted to jump to
3♣, preparing to support spades on the next round, but jumping in clubs
and then bidding spades is consistent with holding four clubs and only
three spades – another fine example of bidding round the houses. This
hand is much better than the previous example – a full trick better to be
precise – and for game to have no reasonable play partner will have to be
missing both the top two spade honours and the top two diamond honours.
So, clearly, the hand is full value for a raise to game but having said that it
must be more helpful to partner to paint a more detailed picture of your
hand if it is at all possible. By jumping to 4♣, which can barely be natural,
we convey the message of a full weight raise to 4♠ including a club control.
If partner has a diamond control, he might just be able to consider bidding
a slam.

For example, partner might hold as little as:

♠ AK975
♡ 862
◇ 5
♣ 9742

and 6♠ is excellent but reverse his minor suit holdings and the slam has
no chance. The *advance-cuebid* of 4♣ makes it easier to explore slam
possibilities at both a lower and safer level.

5.   ♠ Q104
                                      ♡ AQJ742
                                      ◇ AJ3
                                      ♣ 2

Recommended Bid: 3♡

With only fourteen high card points, many players would not think of
jumping to 3♡ on this type of hand; however, the hand is much improved
by the subsidiary fit in spades. If partner has as little as:

♠ KJ65
♡ 93
◇ K865
♣ 765

the heart game is excellent but turn the black suits round and even 2♡ is
not certain to succeed.

OPENER'S REBID: QUIZ II

On each of the following hands, you open 1◇ and your partner responds 1♠, what is your rebid?

1. ♠ A53
    ♡ 7
    ◇ AJ1065
    ♣ K872

2. ♠ A53
    ♡ 7
    ◇ AK1065
    ♣ K872

3. ♠ A53
    ♡ 7
    ◇ AK1065
    ♣ AQ72

4. ♠ AQ3
    ♡ 7
    ◇ AK1065
    ♣ AQ72

5. ♠ A53
    ♡ AQ72
    ◇ AK1065
    ♣ 7

6. ♠ 75
    ♡ AKJ5
    ◇ AQ643
    ♣ Q5

7. ♠ Q53
    ♡ AJ
    ◇ AK1065
    ♣ KQ7

8. ♠ 5
    ♡ AJ5
    ◇ AKQ753
    ♣ K104

ANSWERS TO OPENER'S REBID: QUIZ II

On each of the following hands, you open 1 ◇ and your partner responds 1 ♠, what is your rebid?

1.

♠ A53
♡ 7
◇ AJ1065
♣ K872

Recommended Bid: 2♠

When you opened 1 ◇, you might well have expected to hear a 1 ♡ response – in which case your natural rebid would have been 2♣, showing the expected 5-4 shape in the minors. Many of you will be tempted to make exactly the same rebid here however this would not be the choice of most experts. They choose to rebid 2♠. Why?

As we have already seen, it is quite acceptable to support partner at minimum level with only three trumps especially with a top honour in the trump suit and a singleton in a side suit. Indeed, with a minimum opener, it is your duty to support your partner if you can.

Let's put it another way. Suppose that you do decide to rebid 2♣ and your partner gives you preference to 2 ◇, wouldn't it be tempting to continue with 2♠? For sure, you will have got over your shape but you would also have contravened the principle of supporting as soon as possible with a minimum hand. Therefore your partner will expect you to have this shape *and* some extra values.

Hopefully, the whole picture will become clear as you consider the next three examples:

2.

♠ A53
♡ 7
◇ AK1065
♣ K872

Recommended Bid: 2♣

This time you have a rather better hand. Admittedly this is only two points more than the previous example, but now, if we rebid 2♣ and support spades on the next round, we will not only deliver the expected 3-1-5-4 shape but also the extra values consistent with volunteering to make three bids.

3.
                          ♠ A53
                          ♡ 7
                          ◇ AK1065
                          ♣ AQ72

Recommended Bid: 2♣

Many players would be tempted to jump to 3♣ on this hand as they have substantially more than a minimum opening. However in standard methods this jump into a new suit at the three level not only forces partner to bid again, it is forcing to game. Facing a poor six or seven count trying for nine tricks in no trumps or ten in spades may well be beyond our compass.

At least equally to the point, if you rebid 2♣ it is actually very difficult to construct a hand where game is a good prospect and partner won't bid again even if all he can manage to do is give you preference back to 2◇.

In our previous example, you rebid 2♣ and then bid 2♠ over 2◇. In this case, you are clearly about one trick better, so, after preference to 2◇, you should jump to 3♠. Even this is not absolutely forcing but it does show a hand of about this strength, too good to advance with just 2♠ but not quite strong enough to force to game, facing what might be a totally minimum responding hand. With such a good description of your hand, your partner ought to be able to judge what to do.

4.
                          ♠ AQ3
                          ♡ 7
                          ◇ AK1065
                          ♣ AQ72

Recommended Bid: 3♣

This hand is that little bit stronger again. With nineteen high card points you should have some prospect of making game even if partner is totally minimum. So, this time, jump to 3♣ straightaway, forcing to game. Obviously, your plan should be to support spades on the next round which will complete an excellent picture of your hand.

As you can now see, these first four examples all feature hands with the same 3-1-5-4 shape but they vary in strength right through the spectrum from the minimum to the maximum for a one level opener. Notice that for each step up in strength there is a slightly stronger treatment available. In fact, even quite sophisticated strong club style bidders might be surprised to see just how much definition is available sometimes in good old fashioned natural methods.

5.   ♠ A53
                                ♡ AQ72
                                ◇ AK1065
                                ♣ 7

Recommended Bid: 2♡

Here we have another hand with that attractive 5-4-3-1 shape, still with three card spade support but this time with four hearts rather than four clubs. In fact, it is the same shape as the hand that occupied the first three pages of this chapter – the difference is that this hand is much stronger, certainly strong enough to bid 2♡, a reverse, planning to support spades on the next round.

The name 'reverse' comes from the fact that we have bid our suits in such an order that partner will be forced a level higher just to put us back into our first bid suit. After 1♡-1♠-2◇ responder can give preference to 2♡ without raising the level of the auction but after 1◇-1♠-2♡ responder has to bid 3◇ to give preference. This simple fact is the reason why it is necessary to have a strong hand before reversing.

Now is a good time to deal with one of the perennial hot chestnuts of bidding theory. A large group of classical Acolites will insist that, while a reverse shows a good hand, it is not actually forcing. Contrast this with the view of the modern scientists who insist that a reverse bid should be forcing for one round at least.

As a reverse might conceal up to say twenty or twenty-one points and a shapely hand, passing a reverse is likely to be a very risky business – certainly not a venture to be entered into without a full understanding of what you are doing. Having said that, I would still reserve the right to choose to pass the reverse bid despite those risks. Suppose, for example, you held:

                                ♠ J8742
                                ♡ J93
                                ◇ –
                                ♣ Q9842

Partner opens 1◇ and it is over to you. Would you pass 1◇ and leave partner to his likely doom or take the risk of getting far too high by responding 1♠? I confess, despite my lack of high card points, I would risk responding 1♠; after all, it is not that difficult to construct a hand where 4♠ is much more likely to make than 1◇! However, when I then hear my partner continue with 2♡ I would take the view that the time had come to risk a pass before we hit the stratosphere. Admittedly we might still be lay down for 4♠ but it really isn't that likely and 2♡ figures to be a much, much better contract than 1◊.

6.

♠ 75
♡ AKJ5
◊ AQ643
♣ Q5

Recommended Bid: 1NT

Once again, we have five diamonds and four hearts and rather more than a minimum opening bid. So just like the last hand we could reverse into 2♡, but I would not recommend it. While many partnerships have a way for the responder to show a minimum hand after a reverse, in practice the 2♡ rebid figures to carry your side into game every time responder has a good seven or eight points.

So, is there any alternative? Yes, provided you are playing a weak no trump, you could rebid 1NT to show a balanced 15-17. I would have to agree that this hand is not really balanced but the ♣Q is likely to have more value in no trumps than in suit play, and there is no real risk of either missing a game or even a heart fit. If responder has four hearts, he must have at least five spades and after a 1NT rebid we can be confident that with that shape he will bid his hearts.

Clearly, this option of rebidding 1NT is not available if you are playing a strong no-trump. However, if you think ahead, you might have decided to open 1NT and not 1◊.

7.

♠ Q53
♡ AJ
◊ AK1065
♣ KQ7

Recommended Bid: 2NT

Back to a more mundane balanced hand. With nineteen high card points, were you still tempted to jump to 3NT? I hope not, at least not any more. Remember, whether you are playing a range of 12-14 or 15-17 for your 1NT opener, a jump rebid of 2NT is plenty on this type of hand. Apart from the obvious advantage of being able to stop out of game facing a really weak hand, there is a much more significant advantage in that rebidding 2NT gives much more room to explore which game you want to play in. For example, suppose that partner actually holds:

♠ KJ876
♡ 972
◇ 42
♣ A94

Clearly, if you have jumped to 3NT he will have a totally blind guess as to whether to continue with 4♠ or pass, and most players would chose the latter option. However, over the 2NT rebid there is room to explore to see whether the opener has three card spade support. If responder continues with 3♣ (showing where his outside values actually are) opener will bid 3♠ and responder has a comfortable raise to 4♠.

Fair enough, 3NT will make most of the time but, whenever the opponents lead hearts and a hand with five hearts also has the ♠A, 3NT will fail, while 4♠ will be a make the vast majority of the time.

8.   ♠ 5
                                                ♡ AJ5
                                                ◇ AKQ753
                                                ♣ K104

Recommended Bid: 3NT

Now this is a hand where many will be tempted to make a jump rebid in diamonds. Far be it from me to suggest that this is not the right action, but I would much prefer to jump to 3NT on this type of hand. With a couple of diamonds opposite and some sort of spade stopper nearly any other high card will give 3NT good play. ♠J10xx and the ♣A would be a particularly suitable holding but there is a myriad of hands where 3NT will be an excellent contract and partner will not be close to making another bid after a 3◇ rebid.

Once again, you should appreciate the power of those long diamonds: the fifth and sixth cards in the suit may not have a value under the old Milton Work Point Count but they definitely have a value at the table where you expect they will take two tricks.

OPENER'S REBID: QUIZ III

This time you open 1♠, and your hear partner respond 2♡, what do you rebid now?

1. ♠ AQJ75
    ♡ Q62
    ◇ K72
    ♣ 64

2. ♠ AQJ75
    ♡ Q62
    ◇ A742
    ♣ 6

3. ♠ KQ10942
    ♡ J5
    ◇ AQJ4
    ♣ 7

4. ♠ AKQ42
    ♡ K102
    ◇ 1073
    ♣ A5

5. ♠ AKQ74
    ♡ AQ74
    ◇ 742
    ♣ 2

6. ♠ AKQ74
    ♡ K742
    ◇ 75
    ♣ KQ

ANSWERS TO OPENER'S REBID: QUIZ III

This time you open 1♠, and your hear partner respond 2♡, what do you rebid now?

1.
        ♠ AQJ75
        ♡ Q62
        ◇ K72
        ♣ 64

Recommended Bid: 3♡

A boring minimum opening bid with a good five card spade suit and three card support for partner. A straightforward hand? Evidently not, for over the years well over 50% of players attending my courses have chosen to rebid their spades while about 40% have supported their partner, raising to 3♡. I won't dwell on the much more exotic choices of the missing 10% but concentrate on the major issue.

The response of 2♡ normally shows a five card suit, so as opener you have a duty to announce your knowledge of an eight card fit immediately. If you rebid 2♠ you might get the chance to show your heart support on the next round but there again you might not. Do you really want to insist on playing in 2♠ and find your partner with something like:

        ♠ 6
        ♡ KJ8732
        ◇ A43
        ♣ 975

Well, I suppose that you might if you are a masochist, but with these cards 4♡ is basically dependent on the spade guess and your partner should leave you to fester in 2♠. Of course, I understand that it is tempting to rebid those spades – after all you can actually see what you have in your own hand – but the art of good bidding is based on building up the picture of the combined holdings of the two hands.

2.
        ♠ AQJ75
        ♡ Q62
        ◇ A742
        ♣ 6

Recommended Bid: 4♡

Once again you have three card support for partner but, in reality, you have a much better hand than in our first example. Admittedly you only have one more high card point, but, in the overall context of the hand, the ◊ A is worth a lot more than just one point more than the king and the singleton club gives you both additional control and ruffing value. Now why is the ◊ A so much better than the king. It's not just the fact that the ace is a sure trick but rather more that it is likely to give you more time to get the spades going before you lose any tricks in diamonds.

So, if this is a much better hand than the bare twelve count depicted in our first example, we owe it to our partner to show him that we have extra values by jumping to 4♡ rather than making the same, tame 3♡ bid.

3.   ♠ KQ10942
                                      ♡ J5
                                      ◊ AQJ4
                                      ♣ 7

Recommended Bid: 3♠

Now, here is a good hand for trapping both overbidders who tend to bid 3◊ and underbidders who stolidly bid 2♠.

Let's start with the overbidders. You must remember that if you introduce a new suit at the three level, you have committed your side to playing in game. After all, even *you* would hesitate to criticise your partner for responding 2♡ on something like:

                                      ♠ 53
                                      ♡ KQ987
                                      ◊ K53
                                      ♣ K642

Over 3◊ he is bound to bid 3NT – which has absolutely no chance on the marked club lead. Admittedly 4♠ is much better than 3NT facing this hand, but are you really going to remove 3NT to 4♠ and risk finding partner with a singleton or void spade?

Then the underbidders. If you just count your points you might think that you have little more than a minimum opener, but, be fair, you do have quite a good hand for playing in spades! If you content yourself with just 2♠ you can't really blame your partner for not moving on with a hand like:

♠ J5
♡ KQ987
◇ 1053
♣ A98

when 4♠ is virtually laydown. So what is to be done?

The simple solution is to jump to 3♠ – a bid which is natural and invitational in traditional Acol methods. Notice that your hand has been improved by your partner's response of 2♡ – with Jx in clubs and a singleton heart the hand would clearly not be worth a jump to 3♠.

The invitational jump rebid after a two level response is a bid that has been much maligned by the pseudo-scientists in recent years. Nobody argues against using the jump rebid in this manner after a one level response. On average, if you open 1◇ and jump to 3◇ after a response in one of the majors, you will be showing a good six card suit and about sixteen points. The pseudo-scientists will then argue that with sixteen points and a good six card suit you will normally want to go to game facing a two level response; thus, the jump rebid should be treated as forcing. That all sounds more than reasonable, but no one ever said that a jump rebid facing a two level response should show sixteen points in the first place. If a two level response shows more values than a one level response, it should follow that you need correspondingly less to make an invitational jump rebid after a two level response.

If you choose to play it as invitational in the traditional manner then you should be making the bid with hands like the one in our example. If you choose to play the bid as forcing then, clearly, you should have a better hand.

My view is that retaining the bid in its traditional manner, as non-forcing after a two level response, is particular helpful in judging whether to stretch to good fitting, low point count games. On the stronger types you can normally make do, either by inventing a suit at the three level or by just blasting game.

4.   ♠ AKQ42
                                      ♡ K102
                                      ◇ 1073
                                      ♣ A5

Recommended Bid: 4♣

In my experience very few players have any doubt that this hand is full value for a jump to 4♡. However, if we are going to jump to game on hand two can't we find a way of getting the message through to partner that we actually have a very good raise to 4♡ and not just one based on a bit of good-looking distribution. After all, partner needs very little more than ♡AQxxx and the ◇A to give a heart slam good play, but we cannot afford to propel the auction higher than 4♡ on our own just in case the hands fit badly. Indeed, we might even struggle to make 4♡ if partner has three low diamonds as well.

So, what is to be done? The answer is to jump to 4♣, a cuebid to show control in clubs and a good raise to 4♡. Whatever else it may be, there is absolutely no need for this bid to be natural as you would rebid 3♣ (game forcing) with a strong hand with spades and clubs. Hence, the jump to 4♣ can be used to agree partner's suit and set the slam investigation rolling.

Think about it! What does it cost you? If your partner makes a return cuebid of 4◇, you can put the brakes on by signing off in 4♡. Partner should know that you have a good raise to 4♡ with a club control but you are not that good as you signed off over his 4◇ cuebid.

5.   ♠ AKQ74
                                ♡ AQ74
                                ◇ 742
                                ♣ 2

Recommended Bid: 4♣

While this hand has a point less in high cards, it has considerably more potential than the last example, the singleton club and the fourth trump combine to add enormous playing strength. Now you might be in the slam zone even if partner has a totally minimum 2♡ response. ♡Kxxxx and the ◇A will probably give you excellent play for twelve tricks. However, there is still plenty of room for partner to have a sound 2♡ response while your opponents have three cashing minor suit winners. So, what is to be done?

Once again, you should jump to 4♣ to show control of that suit and a good raise to 4♡. The only difference is that, this time, if partner cuebids 4◇ I would bid more than 4♡. (Playing standard Blackwood, I would settle for a 4♠ cuebid, and if I was fortunate enough to be playing Five Ace Blackwood, where the king of trumps counts as an ace, I would invest in 4NT.)

6.   ♠ AKQ74
                                                 ♡ K742
                                                 ◇ 75
                                                 ♣ KQ

Recommended Bid: 4♣

Once again you hold a very good raise to 4♡, and you would like to express your strength without prcpelling your side too high. My solution would be to bid 4♣ once again.

Now, the last three example hands combine well to illustrate two important principles:

1. There is no space in our methods to incorporate the Gerber 4♣ ace-asking convention when we are considering playing in a suit contract. With the best will in the world, neither Gerber or Blackwood will help us to locate distributional controls, i.e. singletons and voids, which are of great importance in suit contracts. Before pushing our side too high in the search for the slam bonus, it is essential to be able to establish that we at least have some form of control in all of the side suits. The only sensible way of doing this is to adopt some form of cuebidding. Using the unnecessary jump to 4♣ as a cuebid is an essential part of our armoury. To use a golfing analogy, there is not much point in carrying four different wooden clubs in your bag if it means that there is no room for a putter.

2. If you like your advance cuebids to guarantee the ace in the suit bid, or if you prefer to confine the use of one of these jumps to being a splinter, then I hope that these last three examples will help to persuade you to change your mind. Adopt a less rigorous style, use these bids to guarantee a control in the suit, any control – the ace or king, singleton or void. After all, there is nothing to stop you using Blackwood on the next round to make sure that you are not missing two aces. Indeed, it is the fact that Blackwood doesn't really interfere with cuebidding that makes Blackwood in some shape or form the popular choice of ace-asking convention amongst the experts.

4

RESPONDER'S REBID

Let's start our discussion by considering the following awkward hand:

♠ AJ4
♡ KJ1074
♢ AJ
♣ 652

1♢	1♡
1♠	?

With a solid fourteen points facing an opening bid it should be quite clear that we want to be in game, but which one?

First of all, given the information that we have so far, there is no certainty as to which strain we want to play in, let alone at what level. Let's consider some of the alternatives:

1. No Trumps

3NT may be the most likely destination, but there is no guarantee that your opponents will not be able to take the first five tricks, especially with the lead going through partner's club holding. Let's suppose that the whole layout is like this:

♠ KQ65   N   ♠ AJ4
♡ 65   W   E   ♡ KJ1074
♢ KQ1095   S   ♢ AJ
♣ K7   ♣ 652

Played from the West seat, 3NT would be very unlucky to go down. As you have nine top tricks as soon as you get in, South would have to have the ♡A and North the ♣A, and North would have to find the inspired lead of a heart to put South in to lead a club through – a defence that is most unlikely.

2. Hearts

Of course, partner might still hold three card heart support, but, even if he only has a doubleton, 4♡ could still be the right destination. For example, suppose that your combined hands are:

♠ K652
♡ Q5
♢ KQ1095
♣ Q7

♠ AJ4
♡ KJ1074
♢ AJ
♣ 652

For sure, partner really does have a moth-eaten opener but, despite that, 4♡ is still a fair contract. If the opponents attack clubs early, all you will need to do is ruff the third round in the dummy. If the defence is less aggressive, you will be forced to play off three rounds of diamonds before drawing trumps. Of course, you may go down if diamonds are not 3-3 but all other game contracts are considerably worse.

3. Spades

Now suppose that your combined assets are:

♠ KQ109
♡ A
♢ K8752
♣ 1043

♠ AJ4
♡ KJ1074
♢ AJ
♣ 652

On this layout 3NT will fail more than half the time. You will go down either if the opponents take the first five club tricks or if the ♡Q doesn't drop doubleton and the diamond finesse is wrong. Meanwhile, all you need to make 4♠ is for neither opponent to hold a singleton or void in either red suit. Whatever they lead, you should be able to cash two hearts, two diamonds and ruff two of your diamonds with dummy's high trumps making ten tricks in all.

4. Diamonds

While this strain might be the furthest from your mind, once it transpires that partner has a six card diamond suit, playing in diamonds becomes a definite possibility. For example look at this layout:

♠ K652
♡ A5
♢ KQ10965
♣ 8

♠ AJ4
♡ KJ1074
♢ AJ
♣ 652

See how this hand will play in diamonds. Ruff the the second club, cash the ♡AK and ruff a heart high. If the ♡Q was doubleton or hearts are 3-3, you will already be able to claim twelve tricks. Failing that, ruffing another heart and taking the spade finesse might still yield a small slam bonus and that is facing not that much more than a minimum opener.

All this proves nothing except that we do not really have any idea of the best final destination and we can't sensibly find out without having some way of getting partner to describe his hand further. After all, without some such device what are we going to bid? In this modern age, a jump to either 3♡ or 3♠ would not be regarded as forcing and, from the foregoing discussion, it should be fairly clear that it is a total guess if we just decide to bid a game. Never fear, there is an elegant and particularly useful solution.

The modern style is to play a bid of the fourth suit as forcing, saying: 'At this stage, partner, I cannot make an accurate bid to describe my hand. Would you, please, describe your hand further and then I may be able to make a more definitive bid on the next round.' The bid of the fourth suit does not promise any particular holding in that suit.

Of all the conventional bids or treatments that I have played, I would regard 'Fourth Suit Forcing (FSF)' as the most important. Apart from giving an immediate solution to the problem of what we are going to bid next on our example hand, it is a device that considerably broadens the scope and range of ways in which we can describe our own hand.

Just for sake of example, let's consider how the auction might develop on each of our example hands:

1.

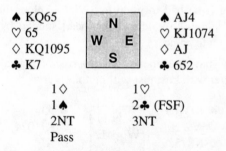

	♠ KQ65		♠ AJ4
	♡ 65		♡ KJ1074
	◇ KQ1095		◇ AJ
	♣ K7		♣ 652

1◇	1♡
1♠	2♣ (FSF)
2NT	3NT
Pass	

Having already shown an opening hand with five diamonds and four spades, West has an easy 2NT rebid after East uses Fourth Suit Forcing. As East knows that his partner has a club stopper and at most two hearts and four spades, 3NT looks like the obvious contract for East to choose.

2.

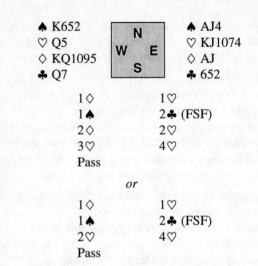

	♠ K652		♠ AJ4
	♡ Q5		♡ KJ1074
	◇ KQ1095		◇ AJ
	♣ Q7		♣ 652

1◇	1♡
1♠	2♣ (FSF)
2◇	2♡
3♡	4♡
Pass	

or

1◇	1♡
1♠	2♣ (FSF)
2♡	4♡
Pass	

West faces an interesting choice between 2◇ and 2♡ after East introduces Fourth Suit Forcing. While there is nothing wrong with showing secondary support for hearts with just ♡Q5, the good texture of the diamond suit would persuade most players to rebid 2◇ at this stage. However, as you can see, you should end up in the right spot either way.

Notice that, after the 2◇ rebid, East has no need to jump the bidding as 2♡ should be forcing. With a weak hand he would not have used the fourth suit bid, and, with only a reasonable five card suit, it would be very space consuming if he had to jump to 3♡ to explore the hand further. West eventually admits to holding some heart support by raising to 3♡ and East presses on to game.

If West admits to having some heart support straightaway, the sequence will be a lot shorter with East just settling for 4♡.

3.

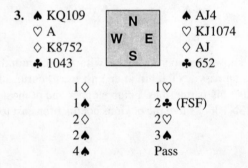

	♠ KQ109		♠ AJ4
	♡ A		♡ KJ1074
	◇ K8752		◇ AJ
	♣ 1043		♣ 652

1◇	1♡
1♠	2♣ (FSF)
2◇	2♡
2♠	3♠
4♠	Pass

West really has no attractive bid after East uses Fourth Suit Forcing. He can barely bid no-trumps with no club stopper, spades without extra length or hearts with only a singleton. East's bid is still forcing, so West has to find yet another bid, but, now, he can emphasise the quality of his spades without any risk of East thinking that he has a five card spade suit as clearly he would have bid 2♠ in response to 2♣.

In a similar way, if East had four spades he would have supported West earlier so now he can bid 3♠ comfortably. With no really sensible alternative, West presses on to the spade game.

4.

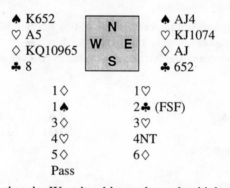

♠ K652	♠ AJ4
♡ A5	♡ KJ1074
◇ KQ10965	◇ AJ
♣ 8	♣ 652

1◇	1♡
1♠	2♣ (FSF)
3◇	3♡
4♡	4NT
5◇	6◇
Pass	

Despite the fact that the West hand has only twelve high card points, my feeling is that the most descriptive bid after the fourth suit 2♣ is 3◇. After all, on the last deal we saw that failing anything else, West would have to rebid 2◇, which means that, 2◇ is essentially a nothing bid. This West hand has a very good diamond suit and is a bit better than minimum whichever way you look at it. You could either argue that the sixth diamond is likely to produce one more trick in the play compared with a five card suit or you could say that many players would still open this hand if the ♠K was replaced with just the ♠J, so you do have a couple of points more than you might have.

East has a slightly awkward rebid at this stage: clearly he has good enough diamond support to consider supporting his partner but, if West has a singleton heart and two clubs; 3NT might still be the only place to play, so East maintains his original intention to repeat his hearts in forcing to game fashion.

Now what should West do? With a singleton club and ♡A5 facing a possible six card suit, 4♡ must be a real possibility. Indeed, as West has already jumped to 3◇, if he now just raises to 4♡ East really should have a good picture of his hand. Clearly, West has shown a 4-2-6-1 distribution with good diamonds, and if East can picture the type of hand he should expect opposite then he could proceed with Blackwood, just to make sure that the partnership is not missing two aces before bidding the slam in diamonds.

All this may seem a little far-fetched, but it does illustrate the type of descriptive bidding that should become available once you have grown accustomed to the use of Fourth Suit Forcing. Quite clearly, regular partnerships will discuss the sequences that might follow Fourth Suit Forcing in some detail. However, at the very least, it gives you a way out of many impossible bidding situations.

Better still, the fourth suit provides a way of describing a whole new tier of hands. For example, suppose that when we bid 2♣ partner obliges by rebidding 2NT, then any suit bid we make at the three level must be forcing.

For example:

1◇	1♡	1◇	1♡
1♠	3♡	1♠	2♣ (FSF)
		2NT	3♡
non-forcing		*forcing*	

1◇	1♡	1◇	1♡
1♠	3◇	1♠	2♣ (FSF)
		2NT	3◇
non-forcing		*forcing*	

Now let's move on and consider what you would do on the following hand:

♠ A6
♡ KJ1074
◇ AJ
♣ J652

1◇	1♡
1♠	?

This time, you have something of a club stopper in principle so, at least, you could take a shot at 3NT – but is there any guarantee that 3NT will be the right contract? I think not.

To start with, partner could possibly still have three card support, and even if he has only two hearts, 4♡ could easily be better than 3NT.

Suppose, that opener holds:

♠ KQJ5
♡ Q5
◇ KQ1087
♣ 72

would you not prefer to play in 4♡? For sure, 4♡ is not laydown, especially if the defence are unkind enough to lead a low heart and duck the first round, but it is a lot better than playing in 3NT and watching the opponents take the first five tricks.

No, once we have decided to add Fourth Suit Forcing to our system, it is much better to employ it on this round and see what partner does before making a final decision. After all, we can always bid 3NT next. To bid 3NT directly over 1♠ should suggest a very good club holding – in principle, two club stoppers. To bid 3NT after using Fourth Suit Forcing suggests less good cover in the fourth-suit.

Now, before putting you to the test with two more quizzes, let's have a look at a different situation:

Responding to Reverses
Consider the following situation:

1♣	1♠
2♡	?

What would you bid next holding either:

(a)	♠ KJ65	*or*	(b)	♠ KJ65
	♡ J72			♡ 765
	◇ 765			◇ K72
	♣ J72			♣ K72

The traditional view is that with hand (a) you should simply give preference to 3♣. This is a weak bid and despite the fact that the opener has shown a good hand by reversing, there is no compulsion for him to bid again after 3♣ unless he has noticeable extra values. Meanwhile, that creates a problem with hand (b) where the only real way ahead is to wheel out the fourth suit bid of 3◇ to create a forcing situation. Thereafter, on the next round, responder can reveal the reason for his enthusiasm should he wish to do so. For example, if opener bids 3NT, should responder call it a day and pass or should he press on with 4♣?

In fact, in good old-fashioned Acol, after:

1♣	1♠
2♡	?

bids of 2♠, 2NT and 3♣ were all regarded as natural and non-forcing and I have even heard some experts say that a jump to 3♠ should be treated the same way. Frankly, this just doesn't make sense.

Clearly, we need to have some way of putting the brakes on but, on many hands, our main interest will be in exploring which is the best game or even whether we have a slam. This is very difficult if the only real way to show any extra values is to introduce the fourth suit.

As a first step, I believe that it is essential to treat a return to opener's suit as showing at least three card support and game-going values, so that on hand (b) above we can bid 3♣ as a first move towards exploring the hand. That all sounds fine but what on earth are we going to bid with hand (a) if 3♣ is natural and forcing?

The answer is that we need to introduce some form of artificial negative to help us handle this situation. In my experience, the bid that most average players seem to consider playing this way is 2NT. I am not suggesting that this is necessarily the best solution but it certainly goes a long way towards improving bidding structure. (In expert circles many players choose to use either the lowest available bid, or a rebid of responders suit in this way.)

Let's look and see how the auction might develop facing one example hand. Suppose opener holds:

♠ 8
♡ AK82
♢ Q8
♣ AQJ1064

Facing hand (a) the whole auction ought to be:

1♣	1♠
2♡	2NT (negative)
3♣	Pass

After the artificial 2NT negative, opener rebids his six card club suit and responder passes. With a game-going hand facing a minimum responding hand opener would have to find a stronger action such as introducing the fourth suit himself.

Facing hand (b) the bidding might be:

1♣	1♠
2♡	3♣ (forcing)
3♢	3NT
Pass	

Knowing of a club fit and game-going values opposite, opener explores the hand by introducing the fourth suit. Having already expressed the value of the hand and shown his club support, responder should have no qualms in bidding 3NT, a sensible final resting place.

Just because 2NT may be an artificial negative does not necessarily mean that you have to bid 2NT with all weak hands, After all, if the main feature of the responding hand is a reasonable five card spade suit, it would make a lot more sense to rebid 2♠ than 2NT. Opener can pass or raise or make another bid as appropriate.

However, this additional option would only be available if responder can rebid his suit at the two level, as a suit rebid at the three level should be treated as unconditionally forcing.

Finally, if opener makes a high level reverse, such as:

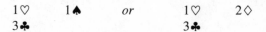

1♡	1♠	*or*	1♡	2♢
3♣			3♣	

it is already game forcing. Thereafter, all bids by responder are aimed at finding the best game or exploring for slam. Similarly, there is much less case for adopting the 2NT negative arrangement if the initial response was at the two level.

RESPONDER'S REBID: QUIZ I

Consider what you would bid next in the following:

1. ♠ Q72
    ♡ K42
    ◇ 86
    ♣ KQJ42

Partner	You
1♡	2♣
2NT*	?

    2NT showed 15-17

5. ♠ AJ742
    ♡ 86
    ◇ KJ5
    ♣ Q105

Partner	You
1♡	1♠
2♣	?

2. ♠ Q42
    ♡ A76
    ◇ Q842
    ♣ J53

Partner	You
1♠	1NT
2NT	?

6. ♠ A105
    ♡ AJ742
    ◇ 1075
    ♣ Q5

Partner	You
1♣	1♡
1♠	?

3. ♠ A10872
    ♡ K72
    ◇ K6
    ♣ 842

Partner	You
1♡	1♠
2◇	?

7. ♠ AK642
    ♡ 105
    ◇ 742
    ♣ AQ10

Partner	You
1♡	1♠
2♡	?

4. ♠ Q10972
    ♡ AQ5
    ◇ 87
    ♣ K42

Partner	You
1♡	1♠
1NT*	?

    1NT showed 15-17

8. ♠ AK1042
    ♡ J5
    ◇ 742
    ♣ K104

Partner	You
1♡	1♠
2♡	?

ANSWERS TO RESPONDER'S REBID: QUIZ I

Consider what you would bid next in the following:

1.
♠ Q72
♡ K42
◇ 86
♣ KQJ42

1♡	2♣
2NT*	?

*Partner's 2NT showed 15-17

Recommended bid: 3♡

We start with a straightforward problem. Clearly we have enough for game but, if partner has five hearts, 4♡ is likely to be a better spot than 3NT, especially if his diamonds are not too strong. How can we find out?

The classic solution to this problem is to bid three of partner's major to offer him a choice of games. If he holds five hearts you expect him to bid 4♡, if not he will bid 3NT.

Note that this type of sequence needs to be distinguished from the jump to three of partner's major when he has bid two suits. On a sequence like 1♠–2♣–2◇, the jump to 3♠ is purely invitational, but, on a sequence where partner rebids in no trumps, three of his suit has to be forcing. When you have bid three suits you can bid the fourth suit to create a forcing situation. When you have only bid two suits, you can't.

2.
♠ Q42
♡ A76
◇ Q842
♣ J53

1♠	1NT
2NT	?

Recommended bid: 3♠

In practice this is a similar sequence to our first example. If you were minimum you would pass 2NT, but, as you are clearly maximum you press on to game. Once you have decided to bid on, 3♠ offers a choice of games. As before, you expect your partner to bid 4♠ with a five card spade suit or 3NT with only four. He should not pass 3♠.

3.   ♠ A10872
                                ♡ K72
                                ◇ K6
                                ♣ 842

            1♡   1♠
            2◇   ?

Recommended bid: 3♡

Now that your partner has rebid 2◇ you know that he has five hearts and four diamonds at least, so your cards are really working. In fact, if your partner holds as little as:

                                ♠ 64
                                ♡ AQ643
                                ◇ AQ75
                                ♣ 95

4♡ is a fair contract that will succeed with no more than reasonable distributions. On the other hand he could have:

                                ♠ 64
                                ♡ J8764
                                ◇ AQJ7
                                ♣ KQ

and 4♡ is a very poor contract. So the right approach is to jump to 3♡ to invite partner to bid the game.

Notice that, when we have already bid three suits, we do not need the jump in the opener's first suit to be forcing and offering a choice of games, because we can always create a forcing situation by bidding the fourth suit first.

4.   ♠ Q10972
                                ♡ AQ5
                                ◇ 87
                                ♣ K42

            1♡   1♠
            1NT*   ?

            *Partner's 1NT shows 15-17

Recommended bid: 3♡

As in our first two examples, this time we have enough to insist on game, but which one? If partner has five hearts, 4♡ should be right; if he has three spades, 4♠ should be right; and if he has neither we will have to settle for 3NT.

As before, after the 1NT rebid the jump to 3♡ is forcing and offers a choice of games. With five hearts opener should press on to 4♡; without five hearts he should bid 3♠ with three spades or 3NT with only two spades.

3♣ is a possible but inferior alternative because at the very least it should locate a 5-3 spade fit. With a game going hand with five spades but only two hearts responder is a little stuck for a bid, as the immediate 3♠ rebid is consistent with an invitational strength hand with six spades. Accordingly to find the 5-3 spade fit responder has to 'invent' a suit at the three level to try and get preference to spades. Over the pseudo-natural 3♣ bid, opener should bid 3♠ with three or else make an alternative descriptive bid, provided that he does not go past 3NT. If his hearts are good and he is relatively weak in diamonds he may bid 3♡, so the 5-3 heart fit will not always be lost.

5.
             ♠ AJ742
             ♡ 86
             ◇ KJ5
             ♣ Q105

        1♡   1♠
        2♣   ?

Recommended bid: 2NT

With good cover in the fourth suit it is right to bid no trumps yourself rather than pass the buck, and as partner has not guaranteed holding more than twelve high card points (and on a bad day he may have less!), there is no need to bid more than 2NT. This is a limit bid and, like all other limit bids, partner may pass or press on to game with a couple of points to spare.

6.
       ♠ A105
       ♡ AJ742
       ♢ 1075
       ♣ Q5

    1♣   1♡
    1♠   ?

Recommended bid: 2♢

This time, without Fourth Suit Forcing you would really have a problem. You have an invitational strength hand without enough black cards to support either of partners suit in invitational manner. A jump to 3♣ would show invitational strength and three card support, while a jump to 3♠ would show the same sort of values but with four card spade support.

Once you have decided to adopt Fourth Suit Forcing you can solve this problem by bidding 2♢. Note that, if your partner just bids 2NT, you can pass for your 2♢ bid guaranteed at least invitational values so with a good looking fourteen point hand with a good diamond holding your partner could, and should, have jumped to 3NT.

It might be worth noting at this stage that, while some modernist players choose to play Fourth Suit Forcing as game forcing, the traditional style is to regard the use of Fourth Suit Forcing at the one or two level as guaranteeing just invitational values, while using the fourth suit at the three level is forcing to game. Indeed, bidding any 'new suit' at the three level should regarded as game forcing.

7.
       ♠ AK1042
       ♡ 105
       ♢ 742
       ♣ AQ10

    1♡   1♠
    2♡   ?

Recommended bid: 3♣

With a trim looking thirteen high card points facing an opening bid, it is fairly clear that you should play this hand in game, but if you had to choose which game to play in at this stage you could easily get it wrong. So bid 3♣ and see what partner has to say.

Note straightaway that, if opener has five hearts and four clubs, you would have expected him to rebid 2♣ rather than 2♡, so there is no real danger of him supporting your 'club suit' at this stage. Even if he does support clubs now then he must have very good hearts so you put him back to 4♡ in comfort.

Also note that over 3♣ opener has a wide choice of possible actions. He could repeat his hearts with a good suit (and you will have a comfortable raise to 4♡), he could support spades (and you will try 4♠) or with a good diamond holding he can bid 3NT. With none of these he can fall back on our new found friend by bidding 3◊, Fourth Suit Forcing!

8.

> ♠ AK1042
> ♡ J5
> ◊ 742
> ♣ K104

1♡	1♠
2♡	?

Recommended bid: 3♡

While your hand does have some promising features, you really do not have enough to commit your side to game but that doesn't mean that game is not on. While 3♣ would indicate where your minor suit values actually are, it is an overbid as it is forcing to game. So what is to be done?

The choice lies between an invitational 2NT and an invitational raise to 3♡. As partner should have either a six card suit or five good hearts, so the raise to 3♡ seems to fit the bill.

RESPONDER'S REBID: QUIZ II

On every one of the following examples, your partner opens 1♠, you respond 2♣ and partner rebids 2♡. What do you do next?

1. ♠ J4
    ♡ Q72
    ◇ Q72
    ♣ AJ1062

5. ♠ 74
    ♡ KJ62
    ◇ 84
    ♣ AJ1064

2. ♠ Q4
    ♡ J42
    ◇ Q74
    ♣ AKJ64

6. ♠ Q4
    ♡ KJ62
    ◇ 84
    ♣ AJ1064

3. ♠ Q4
    ♡ J4
    ◇ Q1074
    ♣ AKJ64

7. ♠ 74
    ♡ KJ62
    ◇ A4
    ♣ AJ1064

4. ♠ AJ3
    ♡ Q4
    ◇ K74
    ♣ A10965

8. ♠ K4
    ♡ KJ62
    ◇ 84
    ♣ AQJ104

ANSWERS TO RESPONDER'S REBID: QUIZ II

On every one of the following examples, your partner opens 1♠, you respond 2♣ and partner rebids 2♡. What do you do next?

1.
♠ J4
♡ Q72
◊ Q72
♣ AJ1062

Recommended bid: 2♠

This is a slightly awkward hand. Add the ◊ J and most players would happily continue with 2NT, but as it is the hand is not quite strong enough to make an invitational bid in no-trumps and the diamond holding isn't really solid enough either. On the other hand, passing 2♡ would be a very dangerous position to take, as if partner has anything in the region of fifteen or sixteen points your expectation would be that you should be in game.

The answer here is to give false preference to 2♠ – after all, our expectation is that opener has at least five spades and four hearts, so if he does pass 2♠ it should prove to be a playable spot. Meanwhile, the real hope is that partner will have sufficient values to drum up another bid so that we can reach game.

2.
♠ Q4
♡ J42
◊ Q74
♣ AKJ64

Recommended bid: 3◊

This time you clearly have sufficient values to expect to make game. Of course, many players would simply gamble out 3NT but, facing a small singleton diamond or even a doubleton, it is all too likely that 3NT is not the right spot. Once again, the solution is to fall back on 3◊, Fourth Suit Forcing. If opener rebids 3♡, showing at least 5-5 in the majors, you have an easy raise to 4♡, if opener rebids 3♠ suggesting a six card suit or stressing a good five carder then you raise to 4♠ and if opener bids 3NT you are happy to pass, and just as a useful bonus if he has ◊ Kx you will be playing 3NT from the right side.

3.

♠ Q4
♡ J4
◇ Q1074
♣ AKJ64

Recommended bid: 3NT

An easy one this time. With game-going values and a potential double-stopper in diamonds, you bid 3NT – what else?

4.

♠ AJ3
♡ J4
◇ K74
♣ A10965

Recommended bid: 3◇

This is another game going hand where you have a pretty good idea of where you want to play. Partner is known to have five spades so 4♠ looks like an excellent spot. Accordingly, many players would succumb to the temptation to bid 4♠ straightaway but, in my view, that would be a mistake.

If you remember, way back in Chapter 2, we introduced the concept of a Delayed Game Raise, so if you bid 4♠ now your partner will probably expect you to deliver a decent five card club suit and four card trump support. To avoid over exciting your partner, wheel out 3◇ Fourth Suit Forcing again, planning to support spades on the next round.

Sometimes this style can yield a really unexpected bonus; for example consider this layout:

```
        ♠ KQ752        N        ♠ AJ3
        ♡ A10954    W     E     ♡ Q4
        ◇ A5           S        ◇ K74
        ♣ 7                     ♣ A10965
```

The whole auction might even be:

1♠	2♣
2♡	3◇ (FSF)
3♡	3♠ (i)
4◇ (ii)	5♣ (iii)
5♡ (iv)	6◇ (v)
6♠ (vi)	Pass

(i) Opener's convenient 3♡ rebid left room for East to show his spade support at the three level.

(ii) With a fairly good hand West takes the opportunity to show some extra values by cuebidding 4◇.

(iii) All of a sudden this routine game-going hand looks a lot more interesting. If partner has 5-5 in the majors and the ◇A, then East already knows that there are no minor suit losers. Even if West has two small clubs, the ◇K will provide a discard. East should surely expect West to have some extra values for his mild slam try, and nine or ten points in the majors would still only give West thirteen or fourteen points. However, East has seven points in the majors himself – so at worst it would appear that East/West are missing only three or four points in the majors, and most of the time that will mean only one major suit loser. So, even without any more information, East should be able to 'see' that 6♠ is a likely final destination. In fact, it would not be ridiculous for East to bid the slam at this stage, but cuebidding 5♣ at least gives West a chance to back-pedal with poor holdings in the majors.

(iv) With no wasted values West cooperates with a further cuebid of 5♡.

(v) From East's point of view it is unclear that West would have bid any differently with:

> ♠ KQ752
> ♡ AKJ52
> ◇ A5
> ♣ 7

when the grand slam should be easy, so East makes a clear-cut grand slam try making yet another cuebid.

(vi) Without the ♡K West has little option but to sign off in 6♠.

I hope that the message is clear: in many situations Fourth Suit Forcing provides the extra space needed to really explore a hand.

5.

> ♠ 74
> ♡ KJ62
> ◇ 84
> ♣ AJ1064

Recommended bid: 3♡

While this is a very much a minimum hand for a 2♣ response there is no question of passing the opener's 2♡ rebid. After all if partner holds as little as:

(a) ♠ AK862
♡ AQ53
◇ 65
♣ 53

game is excellent, but facing a rather less suitable hand:

(b) ♠ KJ986
♡ A1075
◇ KQ
♣ 53

even 3♡ is likely to prove to be a struggle. So, responder should raise to 3♡ and leave the final decision to opener.

Both hand (a) and hand (b) contain thirteen high card points but with hand (a) opener should accept the invitation, while with hand (b) he should most surely decline. The real difference is that hand (a) has good controls and crisp values with really nothing wasted in terms of playing in hearts. while hand (b) lacks top controls and has much slower values. The doubleton ◇KQ is a particularly poor holding: one quick loser but only one trick. Adding another diamond and taking away a club would leave West with a much better hand.

6.   ♠ Q4
♡ KJ62
◇ 84
♣ AJ1064

Recommended bid: 4♡

This is a much better hand. Notice that even facing hand (b) 4♡ depends on little more than finding the queen of trumps. The real difference is not just that the ♠Q is two more points but that the additional queen is known to be in a key suit. So responder should leave nothing to chance by raising to 4♡.

7.   ♠ 74
♡ KJ62
◇ A4
♣ AJ1064

Recommended bid: 4◇

It should be reasonably clear that this is a much better hand than our last example, and if that hand was worth a raise to game this hand has some considerable slam potential, but you would not want to get too high facing hand (b). Once again, we could use Fourth Suit Forcing and then support hearts to show a better game-going hand but there is a better approach with this type of hand. Jump to 4◇, an advance cuebid showing control in diamonds and a good raise to 4♡.

8.   ♠ K4
                                                   ♡ KJ62
                                                   ◇ 84
                                                   ♣ AQJ104

Recommended bid: 4◇

This hand is by way of contrast with the last example, once again you have a good enough hand to want to show a good raise to 4♡ but as you have no control in diamonds you cannot jump to 4◇. This time settle for bidding a fourth suit 3◇ planning to support hearts on the next round.

RESPONDER'S REBID: QUIZ III

First, consider your choice of action if the bidding has started:

1♦	1♠
2♡	?

1. ♠ KJ1065
    ♡ Q5
    ◇ 75
    ♣ J952

3. ♠ QJ65
    ♡ Q52
    ◇ 75
    ♣ KJ94

2. ♠ KJ1065
    ♡ A5
    ◇ 75
    ♣ J652

4. ♠ QJ65
    ♡ Q5
    ◇ 75
    ♣ J1076

Now suppose instead that the auction starts:

1♡	2◇
2♠	?

What would you bid with each of the following hands:

5. ♠ 75
    ♡ Q65
    ◇ KQJ105
    ♣ Q52

7. ♠ K5
    ♡ AQ5
    ◇ AJ1054
    ♣ 753

6. ♠ K5
    ♡ Q65
    ◇ AJ1054
    ♣ 752

8. ♠ K5
    ♡ 75
    ◇ AQJ976
    ♣ J75

ANSWERS TO RESPONDER'S REBID: QUIZ III

First, consider your choice of action if the bidding has started:

1◇   1♠
2♡   ?

1.
♠ KJ1065
♡ Q5
◇ 75
♣ J952

Recommended bid: 2♠

Without doubt the main feature of this hand is the good five card spade suit, so, without much more than you have already promised, just bid 2♠. If opener cannot drum up another bid you are unlikely to have missed a game and if he does bid again you should be reasonably well placed.

If partner continues with 2NT, 3♣, 3◇ or even 3♡, you would bid 3NT, comfortable in the knowledge that you have already shown a fair spade suit. If partner raises to 3♠, you have enough to press on to game; after all, you might bid exactly the same way without the ♡Q.

2.
♠ KJ1065
♡ A5
◇ 75
♣ J652

Recommended bid: 3♣

This time you have the same shape but clearly you have enough values to commit your side to game. However, with such good spades and relatively poor clubs, it would be a mistake to just jump to 3NT. Bid 3♣, Fourth Suit Forcing, showing that you have game going values but asking your partner to continue describing his hand.

3.
♠ QJ65
♡ Q52
◇ 75
♣ KJ94

Recommended bid: 3NT

With nine high card points facing a reverse, you should be confident of making a game on your combined assets and you have a pretty good idea already of where you want to play. A jump to 3NT gives a good description of your hand.

4.   ♠ QJ65
                                     ♡ Q5
                                     ◊ 75
                                     ♣ J1076

Recommended bid: 2NT

As partner could easily have nineteen or twenty points on this auction, we really have to drum up another bid. Try 2NT, then, if opener bids 3◊, you can sensibly pass. On the other hand, if he continues with either 3♣, Fourth Suit Forcing, or 3♠ you have a comfortable 3NT bid.

Now suppose instead that the auction starts:

1♡	2◊
2♠	?

What would you bid with each of the following hands:

5.   ♠ 75
                                     ♡ Q65
                                     ◊ KQJ105
                                     ♣ Q52

Recommended bid: 3♡

With three card heart support, this hand is just a little too strong to raise to 2♡ on the first round but in choosing to respond 2◊ you should always have been planning to support hearts on the next round. As opener's reverse guarantees a five card heart suit it seems obvious that responder should support hearts now. After the initial two level response, there is no question of 3♡ not being forcing, but, having supported hearts, you should be more than happy to pass if opener continues with 3NT,

6.   ♠ K5
                            ♡ Q65
                            ◇ AJ1054
                            ♣ 752

Recommended bid: 4♡

This hand has the same number of high card points and the same shape
but it has much greater playing potential, much better controls and rather
more high card strength in partner's two suits. With this type of hand, the
recommended Acol style action is to jump to 4♡, to show a fairly minimum,
but highly suitable, hand. The real issue is that with hands of this type you
would feel unhappy if you bid 3♡ and partner just raised to 4♡, for 6♡
could easily be a good contract facing a fairly minimum reversing hand
such as:

                            ♠ A943
                            ♡ AK10742
                            ◇ K7
                            ♣ 8

but you wouldn't really want to bid on, just in case partner produces
something like:

                            ♠ QJ94
                            ♡ AKJ74
                            ◇ KQ
                            ♣ Q5

With eighteen high card points this hand is full value for the reverse but
there are still three obvious top losers if you press on to the five level.

7.   ♠ K5
                            ♡ AQ5
                            ◇ AJ1054
                            ♣ 753

Recommended bid: 3♡

By way of contrast, this is an even stronger hand. This time, when partner
simply raises your 3♡ to 4♡, you would feel confident that you have
enough to risk pressing on to the five level. Personally, I would cuebid
4♠ in the hope of eliciting a club cuebid from opener.

8.

    ♠ K5
    ♡ 75
    ◇ AQJ976
    ♣ J75

Recommended bid: 3◇

Having already responded at the two level, there is no need to do more
than repeat your diamonds to emphasise the quality of your suit. As you
can see, facing a good high card reverse such as:

    ♠ A642
    ♡ AK862
    ◇ K2
    ♣ A4

6◇ is the winning contract and facing:

    ♠ AQ64
    ♡ AK862
    ◇ K2
    ♣ 86

5◇ is undoubtedly the right place to play.

5
PARTSCORE OR GAME

Most players do not experience too much difficulty learning the basic requirements for bidding and making game with two balanced hands. Indeed, one of the early lessons most players learn is that twenty-five high card points is enough to make game, and most no trump bidding is orientated to establishing whether the partnership holds this magic total of twenty-five points or not.

However you look at it, distributional hands are not so easy, but many players will improve dramatically when they come to appreciate that the degree of fit is frequently more important than the point count. It is all very well learning to adjust the point count evaluation to allow for distributional features but most of the time it is an appreciation of the *combined assets* of the two hands that is important and not an individual evaluation.

It is for this simple reason that, in the first half of this book, I have placed so much emphasis on the importance of supporting partner when you have support. Unless he knows the extent of your support for his suit quickly, he will have no chance of applying sensible judgement in the bidding. Now, consider just how many tricks you will make from the following pair of hands:

♠ A5432		♠ K876
♡ A5		♡ 432
◇ A432		◇ K5
♣ 32		♣ 5432

However you look at it, three unsupported aces and no singleton is not that much more than a minimum opening bid and just two kings is not the greatest responding hand, but if spades break 2-2 and the side suits break reasonably most players will soon rattle up ten tricks by ruffing two diamonds in the dummy.

This remarkable result is entirely due to the degree of fit – a nine card trump fit, no wasted values in the honour cards, and the very convenient diamond combination, effectively providing four tricks with the aid of two ruffs.

Now look at what happens if you move the responder's holdings around, consider:

♠ A5432   ♠ K876
♡ A5   ♡ K4
◇ A432   ◇ 765
♣ 32   ♣ 7654

Just switching the red suit holdings clearly costs a trick. Move the K5 into the club suit and, if the ace of clubs is on the wrong side, the total trick count will be right back down to eight; indeed on a bad day when the trumps break 3-1 and the ♣A is wrong you will struggle to make even eight tricks.

So, while it is fairly clear that the total number of trumps is an important factor in determining how many tricks your side can make, it should also be clear that the location of both high cards and shortages is equally important. For example, consider the following pair of hands:

(a) ♠ AQ765   or   (b) ♠ AQ765
    ♡ Q5   ♡ 75
    ◇ AJ52   ◇ AJ52
    ♣ 75   ♣ Q5

You open 1♠ and let us suppose that your partner responds 2♣ but then jumps to 3♠ over your 2◇ rebid. What would you do next?

Of course, with only thirteen high card points and not particularly good distribution, you may be tempted to pass on both hands, but it is fairly clear to me that hand (b) is much better than hand (a), for while the ♡Q figures to be wastepaper the ♣Q is likely to be working hard for you. Your partner could easily have something like:

♠ K42
♡ 982
◇ Q6
♣ AJ864

Facing hand (a) you have two certain heart losers and a club loser and then, even if the diamond finesse is right, you really have very poor prospects of disposing of your fourth diamond. While you can ruff the third round of the suit, you will need to find a very good lie of the cards to allow you to ruff the last diamond.

Meanwhile prospects facing hand (b) are much better. If the club finesse is right, declarer will have the luxury of leading up to the ◇ Q. Even if the ◇ K is over the queen, he will then only need one diamond ruff in the dummy to make his contract. If the club finesse is wrong then declarer will need the diamond finesse to be right, but the club suit will provide a parking place for the fourth diamond.

Accordingly, it seems right to pass with hand (a) and press on to game with hand (b). Is this double dummy? No, I don't think so. It seems commonsense to me to upgrade minor honour cards in the suit that partner has bid and downgrade minor honour cards in the unbid suit. In effect, hand (a) should be re-evaluated at about eleven high card points while hand (b) should be upgraded to about fourteen.

If the decision as to whether to press on to game or not depends on the mesh of high cards and distributional values, it seems sensible that we should use methods that help us to find this out whenever we can. One of the most obvious situations is after partner raises one of a major to two All of which brings us to the subject of Trial bids.

The idea is that, if opener wants to make a game try, he bids the suit where he would most like his partner to be able to help him. Of course, responder is allowed to sign off with a totally minimum hand or bid the game with a maximum hand anyway, but on all the variety of hands that fall somewhere in between he should pay particular attention to his holding in the trial bid suit. He should upvalue his hand if he holds the ace or king of the suit or a singleton or doubleton, and downgrade his hand with holdings like three small. Qxx is clearly much better than three small but it is still not a very good holding; certainly Qx would be much better.

It may seem fairly amazing that we are very close to having enough to make a game try with the hand we started this chapter with, which was:

♠ A5432
♡ A5
◇ A432
♣ 32

Facing the right six point hand, we have already established that game will have reasonable play. On balance, however, making a game try with this hand is a very aggressive action and my assessment would be that you would go down in either 3♠ or 4♠ slightly too often to make the adventure worthwhile. Make the hand just a little bit better and it would be a different story.

So with:

♠ AQ432	*or*	♠ A5432	*or*	♠ A5432
♡ A5		♡ AQ		♡ A5
◇ A432		◇ A432		◇ AQ32
♣ 32		♣ 32		♣ 32

I would make a game try by bidding 3◇ and I would expect my partner to bid 4♠ holding:

♠ K876
♡ 432
◇ K5
♣ 5432

You can work out for yourself just how much better the game is with the addition of a working queen in opener's hand.

By the same token you can see that if the additional queen was in the club suit, the hand would not be worth making the game try.

Now, how would you tackle the following hand:

♠ AJ1054
♡ 1095
◇ AKQ4
♣ 7

You open 1♠ and your partner raises to 2♠, what do you do now? 5-4-3-1 shape hands are always powerful, and you can see that, if partner has just an ace and the king of spades, 4♠ will have fair play, so a game try is called for – but what is that game try going to be?

If the idea is that partner should be able to upvalue his hand when he has a useful holding in the suit that you choose to bid, it should be patently obvious that it is a waste of breath to bid 3◇ – for you really don't need any help in that suit. On the other hand, you would be pleased to find a doubleton heart in the dummy, so you should use 3♡ as your game try.

Now let's look at a slightly different situation. Suppose you find yourself looking at:

♠ AQ764
♡ Q5
◇ Q6
♣ 10762

Your partner opens 1◇, and you respond 1♠ which partner raises to 2♠.

What are your thoughts now?

Many of the players I know would simply pass without giving the hand very much thought, but facing a hand like:

♠ K852
♡ J72
◇ AK1087
♣ 8

4♠ is excellent and you could barely blame the opener for not bidding more than 2♠.

Of course, this responding hand is a little deceptive. The spade holding is excellent and don't forget the power of that fifth trump: the ♡Q is a poor card which might be worth absolutely nothing but the ◇Q looks to be much more valuable as partner has bid the suit. If I was trying to value this hand in the terms of points alone I would add three points for the quality and length of the spades now that opener has supported that suit, deduct one or two for the poor heart holding and add one back on for the diamond holding. So however you look at it this responding hand is worth about twelve high card points and that should be enough to make a game try.

So, what are we going to bid? I would recommend that you bid 3♣ and treat it just like a trial bid. If opener is good for his bidding he might bid the game anyway, and if he is poor he might just go back to 3♠. However, with an in-between hand he should look at his holding in clubs to help him decide. On our example opening hand, opener only has eleven high card points but with a singleton club opposite our length and four card trump support, when he might only have three, he should have no hesitation in accepting your game try.

Alter the opening hand round so that he has a singleton heart and jack to three clubs, then he should definitely reject the game try.

PARTSCORE OR GAME: QUIZ I

You open 1♠ and your partner raises to 2♠.
What do you do with each of the following hands?

1.   ♠ AQ1043
      ♡ KQ5
      ◇ A542
      ♣ 7

2.   ♠ AQ107
      ♡ KQ5
      ◇ A542
      ♣ 75

3.   ♠ AQ105
      ♡ KQ5
      ◇ A75
      ♣ K42

4.   ♠ A109543
      ♡ KQ5
      ◇ A75
      ♣ 7

5.   ♠ A109543
      ♡ AQJ4
      ◇ K5
      ♣ 7

ANSWERS TO PARTSCORE OR GAME: QUIZ I

You open 1♠ and your partner raises to 2♠.
What do you do with each of the following hands?

1.   ♠ AQ1043
                                 ♡ KQ5
                                 ◇ A542
                                 ♣ 7

Recommended Bid: 3◇

This is a good hand, well worth a game try, but to make 4♠ a good contract you would much prefer some help in diamonds to some wasted values in clubs. So bid 3◇.

2.   ♠ AQ107
                                 ♡ KQ5
                                 ◇ KJ42
                                 ♣ 75

Recommended Bid: Pass

Yes, you do have some extra values but really no more than you have promised. After all, if you would have opened 1NT to show 12-14 balanced points then when you open 1♠ with only four spades, you must have at least fifteen points. In terms of playing strength, this hand is really no better than a 5-3-3-2 hand with twelve high card points, so you should pass.

3.   ♠ AQ105
                                 ♡ KQ5
                                 ◇ A75
                                 ♣ K42

Recommended Bid: 2NT

This is a rather better hand which should yield game if partner has seven or eight high card points. Bid 2NT to show a hand of about this strength, then leave the decision to partner; if he has a really weak hand he can still sign off in 3♠.

4.
          ♠ A109543
          ♡ KQ5
          ◇ A75
          ♣ 7

Recommended Bid: 3◇

Only thirteen high card points but the sixth spade is certain to yield an extra trick. Bid 3◇ to help partner to judge whether to bid 4♠ or not.

5.
          ♠ A109543
          ♡ AQJ4
          ◇ K5
          ♣ 7

Recommended Bid: 4♠

Despite the low point count this is a much better hand still. If spades break 2-2 you would have some play for game if all partner has is ♠Kxx. So don't make a game try with this hand, simply bid what you think you can make, 4♠.

PARTSCORE OR GAME: QUIZ II

This time you have the responding hand.
What would you bid after the sequence:

1♠	2♠
3◇	?

1. ♠ K76
    ♡ J753
    ◇ 65
    ♣ Q876

4. ♠ K876
    ♡ J75
    ◇ 765
    ♣ Q76

2. ♠ K76
    ♡ J753
    ◇ K5
    ♣ J876

5. ♠ K876
    ♡ A75
    ◇ 765
    ♣ Q76

3. ♠ K76
    ♡ AJ753
    ◇ 765
    ♣ 86

6. ♠ K876
    ♡ J75
    ◇ Q5
    ♣ 10762

ANSWERS TO PARTSCORE OR GAME: QUIZ II

This time you have the responding hand.
What would you bid after the sequence:

1♠	2♠
3◇	?

1.

♠ K76
♡ J753
◇ 65
♣ Q876

Recommended Bid: 3♠

You have a totally minimum hand for your initial raise to 2♠. Despite the fact that you have a suitable diamond holding you should reject the game try as you only have three spades.

2.

♠ K76
♡ J753
◇ K5
♣ J876

Recommended Bid: 4♠

This time, despite the fact that you only have three card spade support, you should bid 4♠ as your diamond holding could not really be more suitable and one of your outside jacks may make some contribution.

3.

♠ K76
♡ AJ753
◇ 765
♣ 86

Recommended Bid: 3♡

With the king of trumps and an outside ace you have enough to accept the game try despite having the worst possible diamond holding. However, if the opener has three hearts, 4♡ might well be a better contract than 4♠, so bid 3♡ for the moment. If opener raises you to 4♡ that will be a sensible contract, if instead he bids 3♠ you can still raise him to game.

Notice that, despite having a five card heart suit, eight high card points and only three spades, it is right to support spades initially rather than bidding 2♡. The reason is that if you respond 2♡ and partner rebids 2♠ you will be committed to raising to 3♠ in order to show him any spade support – and this is clearly an overbid. It is much better to support spades straightaway hoping to get your hearts with the action later.

4.
    ♠ K876
    ♡ J75
    ◇ 765
    ♣ Q76

Recommended Bid: 3♠

While now you have four card trump support you still have very much a minimum for your raise to 2♠ and your diamond holding really could not be worse. So just bid 3♠ and hope that you have enough for your partner to make it.

5.
    ♠ K876
    ♡ A75
    ◇ 765
    ♣ Q76

Recommended Bid: 4♠

Despite the poor diamond holding, you have a maximum hand for your raise to 2♠. Once again, you have the advantage of holding two key cards so bid 4♠. Note that with only three card spade support and a maximum you could bid 3NT with good holdings in both unbid suits.

6.
    ♠ K876
    ♡ J75
    ◇ Q5
    ♣ 10762

Recommended Bid: 4♠

This time we are back to holding a minimum hand for our initial action but the diamond holding is very suitable and, as we hold four trumps, there is every prospect of ruffing two diamonds in our hand, so bid 4♠. Just see your prospects facing either of the hands which we decided that we should bid 3◇ on in the first quiz, namely:

No 1.   ♠ AQ1043   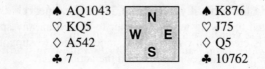   ♠ K876
                 ♡ KQ5   ♡ J75
                 ◇ A542   ◇ Q5
                 ♣ 7   ♣ 10762

Here we have three obvious losers, but if the ◇ K is right, there will be no
difficulty making 4♠ unless the spades break 4-0. If the ◇ K is wrong, we
will need to be a bit more fortunate but if trumps are 2-2 it will be easy to
ruff both losing diamonds in the dummy.

and No 4.   ♠ A109543   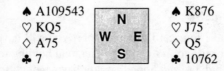   ♠ K876
                 ♡ KQ5   ♡ J75
                 ◇ A75   ◇ Q5
                 ♣ 7   ♣ 10762

With this combination you should have no difficulty making ten tricks
with spades as trumps unless the spades break 3-0 or the defence take an
immediate heart ruff.

PARTSCORE OR GAME: QUIZ III

This time you have a mixture of problems to consider.
First consider what you would do in the following situation:

1♡	1♠
2♠	?

1.   ♠ KQ753
     ♡ Q5
     ◇ K1043
     ♣ 75

2.   ♠ KQ753
     ♡ 75
     ◇ K1043
     ♣ Q5

Then, on each of the following hands what you would do after:

1♡	1♠
3♠	?

3.   ♠ KQ75
     ♡ Q5
     ◇ 753
     ♣ 9652

4.   ♠ KQ75
     ♡ 75
     ◇ 753
     ♣ Q652

Finally, what would you bid after the following sequences with this hand?

     ♠ K543
     ♡ 642
     ◇ Q8642
     ♣ 5

5.   1♠   2♠
             2NT   ?

6.   1♠   2♠
             3♣   ?

7.   1♠   2♠
             3♡   ?

ANSWERS TO PARTSCORE OR GAME: QUIZ III

This time you have a mixture of problems to consider.
First consider what you would do in the following situation:

1♡	1♠
2♠	?

1.

♠ KQ753
♡ Q5
◇ K1043
♣ 75

Recommended Bid: 3◇

An aceless ten count looks like only a marginal candidate for making a game try except for two key attributes:

First, you should expect the fifth spade to be worth a playing trick, and then the ♡Q is well placed to fill a hole in partners suit. If you add one point on for the well-placed queen, even rigid point counters will be making a game try.

2.

♠ KQ753
♡ 75
◇ K1043
♣ Q5

Recommended Bid: Pass

This time, a slightly different story. If you should add a point on for a well-placed queen you should take one off for the poorly placed ♣Q on this hand.

Then consider what you would do after:

1♡	1♠
3♠	?

3.

♠ KQ75
♡ Q5
◇ 753
♣ 9652

Recommended Bid: 4♠

In just the same way here, the well placed queen is well worth an additional point, so you should press on to game.

4.

♠ KQ75
♡ 75
◇ 753
♣ Q652

Recommended Bid: Pass

Just as before, deduct one point for the badly placed ♣Q and you are left with very much a minimum responding hand. If partner can't raise to game, why should you bid on?

Finally, suppose that you hold:

♠ K543
♡ 642
◇ Q8642
♣ 5

then, what do you bid after:

5.

1♠	2♠
2NT	?

Recommended Bid: 3♠

For partner 2NT bid, you should expect partner to hold in the region of a balanced eighteen point hand, something like:

♠ A872
♡ KQ5
◇ AJ7
♣ KJ4

As you can see, even with normal breaks 4♠ would be a real struggle, probably requiring king doubleton in diamonds onside and something favourable in hearts.

6.   1♠   2♠
                         3♣   ?

Recommended Bid: 4♠

Despite your minimum it looks like you have just the right cards for partner. The singleton club is excellent when backed up with four trumps.

7.   1♠   2♠
                         3♡   ?

Recommended Bid: 3♠

With partner looking for help in hearts, three small cards is the worst possible holding.

6
CHOOSING THE BEST GAME

In Chapter Four, we addressed the problem of the responder offering a choice of games and how he might fall back on Fourth Suit Forcing to start exploring for the best game. In this chapter we take a further look at Fourth Suit Forcing and all of its ramifications.

First of all, let's suppose that you are fortunate enough to pick up:

♠ K4
♡ 106
◇ KQ102
♣ AK642

Partner opens 1♠ and you respond 2♣ as we have already established that you don't jump in response with a two-suiter. Rather to your surprise your partner rebids 2◇. What is your next move?

Of course, it is easy to dream of slam, and most players that have attended my classes over the years have been keen to jump to four or even five diamonds. This is all very well but while it is clear that you would like to show interest in a diamond slam, it is not at all clear that even 5◇ will be a good contract if partner has a minimum opening bid. Of course, you want to play in at least game, but couldn't 3NT or 4♠ be a more desirable spot than 5◇?

For example, suppose that the opener has:

♠ AQJ75
♡ Q7
◇ J976
♣ Q7

I would have to agree that this really isn't a great hand but I would be very surprised if more than 5% of regular club players didn't open the bidding with it. Looking at the combined holdings, 5◇ suffers from the obvious embarrassment of three top losers and you would expect the defence to take the first six tricks against 3NT. However, 4♠ is an excellent contract which should succeed unless either the trumps break exceptionally badly or the defence are able to score a quick diamond ruff.

So, rather than leap into the stratosphere, you should start by bidding 2♡, Fourth Suit Forcing, and listen to what partner has to say. Of course your plan is to support diamonds on the next round. If you had four card diamond support and only invitational values, you would have supported diamonds as soon as partner bid them, so using the fourth suit and then supporting diamonds is forcing to game. The real advantage comes because this gives your partner two further opportunities to say something about his hand before you really have to make any decision.

Let's consider how the auction might develop facing four different minimum opening hands, for starters:

(a) ♠ AJ1075   N   ♠ K4
    ♡ Q95   W   E   ♡ 106
    ◇ AJ64   S   ◇ KQ102
    ♣ 5   ♣ AK642

The full sequence:

1♠	2♣
2◇	2♡ (FSF)
2NT	3◇
3♠	4♠
Pass	

Having already shown five spades and four diamonds, opener shows his heart stopper but when responder shows his diamond support opener takes the opportunity to stress the quality of his spades. Having already got the rest of his hand off his chest, responder has a comfortable raise to 4♠.

(b) ♠ AQ753   N   ♠ K4
    ♡ 872   W   E   ♡ 106
    ◇ AJ94   S   ◇ KQ102
    ♣ 7   ♣ AK642

The full sequence:

1♠	2♣
2◇	2♡ (FSF)
2♠	3◇
3♡ (FSF)	3♠
4♠	Pass

With only three small hearts, opener is effectively forced into repeating his spades. Over 3♢, opener returns the compliment by using Fourth Suit Forcing himself, after all, 3NT could be the right contract if responder has any length in hearts. As it happens responder has no help there, but, at least, he can now show his modest spade support. After 3♠, opener raises to game.

(c)   ♠ Q7532   ♠ K4
        ♡ AJ9   **N**   ♡ 106
        ♢ AJ64   **W   E**   ♢ KQ102
        ♣ 5   **S**   ♣ AK642

The full sequence:

1♠	2♣
2♢	2♡ (FSF)
2NT	3♢
3NT	Pass

With a good heart stop and poor spades in a minimum hand, opener responds 2NT to the fourth suit enquiry. When responder reveals his diamond support, opener stresses the good quality of his heart holding by rebidding 3NT. There is no reason for responder to bid on.

(d)   ♠ AJ532   ♠ K4
        ♡ 7   **N**   ♡ 106
        ♢ AJ64   **W   E**   ♢ KQ102
        ♣ Q83   **S**   ♣ AK642

The full sequence:

1♠	2♣
2♢	2♡ (FSF)
3♣	4♢
4♡	4NT
5♡	6♢
Pass	

After Fourth Suit Forcing, West shows his club support. As it is inconceivable that West has more than two hearts, this has the effect of persuading East that 3NT is off the menu. East makes his intentions clear by jumping to 4♢, committing his side to playing in a diamond game or slam.

West's choice of action over this is of considerable interest. As it is possible that he might have bid 3♣ with honour doubleton in clubs, and therefore have two hearts, it seems to me that the most helpful action West could take at this stage is to cuebid 4♡. Confirmation of the hoped for 5-1-4-3 shape is really all East wanted to hear, so he checks for aces and bids the small slam. Notice that 6◇ is a better contract than 6♣ as, if the clubs fail to break, you can still fall back on the spade suit.

One of the noticeable aspects of the first three of these sequences is that, even after responder has shown his strong hand with four card diamond support, the bids below 3NT are aimed at finding the right game rather than being cuebids looking for slam. The same principle should be applied in other situations.

For example, consider your action with the following hand:

♠ QJ5
♡ KQ75
◇ K65
♣ 872

after the auction starts:

1◇	1♡
3◇	?

As partner has shown extra values and a six card diamond suit by making a jump rebid, it is fairly clear that you have enough values to bid game. But which one?

In all fairness, you really do not know. Opener could easily have:

♠ 104
♡ A4
◇ AQJ972
♣ KQ4

when everybody would want to play in 3NT, or he could have:

♠ A104
♡ A42
◇ AQJ972
♣ 4

when you would much prefer to come to rest in 4♡, 5◇ or even 6◇ than play in 3NT and lose the first five club tricks.

So, what is to be done? With insufficient information to make an accurate decision yourself, you have to try and help partner. The way to do this is to show partner where your values lie. In this case, try bidding 3♠.

Note that this bid does not guarantee a four card spade suit and neither is there any legitimate reason for you to be showing five hearts. Pure and simple, you are inviting partner to bid 3NT with a suitable club holding. If he doesn't have a club stopper then he must bid something else.

Then, in a similar vein, consider:

♠ 75
♡ J64
◇ KQ104
♣ J742

Partner opens 1♠, and, naturally enough, you respond 1NT. Now partner jumps to 3♣, what would you do next?

First, as a matter of system, partner's jump to 3♣ should show game-going values with at least five spades and at least four clubs, so we have to bid again. However, at this stage, once again, it is totally unclear which game is going to be best. It could easily be 3NT, 4♠ or 5♣, so what can we do to help partner?

Show him where your values are by bidding 3◇. With a good holding in hearts, he will undoubtedly bid 3NT, with good spades he will probably bid 3♠ and even if he raises diamonds you can go back to 5♣. Indeed, it will be the right contract if he has something like:

♠ AK862
♡ 8
◇ A53
♣ AK96

FINDING THE BEST GAME: QUIZ

For the first three problems,
suppose that you hold the following attractive hand:

♠ 4
♡ 1063
◇ KQ102
♣ AKQJ4

What do you bid, as responder, after the auction has started:

1.
1♠	2♣
2◇	2♡ (FSF)
2NT	3◇
3♠	?

2.
1♠	2♣
2◇	2♡ (FSF)
2♠	3◇
3♡	?

3.
1♠	2♣
2◇	2♡ (FSF)
2NT	3◇
3NT	?

Now suppose that your partner opens 1♣, you respond 1♡
and partner jumps to 3♣. What do you bid next holding:

4.   ♠ J75
      ♡ KJ754
      ◇ AJ6
      ♣ 75

6.   ♠ K75
      ♡ AJ42
      ◇ QJ5
      ♣ 75

5.   ♠ K65
      ♡ AQ1054
      ◇ 542
      ♣ 75

7.   ♠ QJ5
      ♡ A853
      ◇ 9764
      ♣ 75

ANSWERS TO FINDING THE BEST GAME: QUIZ

You hold:

> ♠ 4
> ♡ 1063
> ◊ KQ102
> ♣ AKQJ4

What do you bid next after the following sequences?

1.

1♠	2♣
2◊	2♡ (FSF)
2NT	3◊
3♠	?

Recommended Bid: 3NT

Having been through the Fourth Suit Forcing paraphernalia to show your forcing diamond raise, you are now faced with making a sensible decision. Opener has shown a heart stop and then emphasised his spades. Obviously, you have no interest in playing in spades but, as partner is known to hold a heart stop, why should you look further than 3NT? After all, could you not have three potential heart losers playing in 5◊?

Strangely enough, partner's bidding is totally consistent with a hand we saw much earlier in this chapter, in example (a):

> ♠ AJ1075
> ♡ Q95
> ◊ AJ64
> ♣ 5

2.

1♠	2♣
2◊	2♡ (FSF)
2♠	3◊
3♡	?

Recommended Bid: 3NT

On the previous round partner repeated his spades but now he has used Fourth Suit Forcing himself. Clearly he has heart length but no heart stopper as such, rather like the hand suggested in example (b):

♠ AQ753
♡ 872
◇ AJ94
♣ 7

So, what should you bid over 3♡? You've got it in one, bid 3NT. After all, it is much better to play in 3NT which will succeed as long as the opponents can't cash five heart tricks straightaway than in 5◇ which has three top losers.

3.

1♠	2♣
2◇	2♡ (FSF)
2NT	3◇
3NT	?

Recommended Bid: Pass

This time partner has shown a heart stopper over our Fourth Suit Forcing and emphasised it by bidding 3NT over our 3◇. You have no excuse to bid again!

Now, what do you bid after:

1♣	1♡
3♣	?

4.

♠ J75
♡ KJ754
◇ AJ6
♣ 75

Recommended Bid: 3◇

After our previous discussion, it should seem obvious to bid 3◇, showing enough for game and a diamond stopper for no trump purposes. If opener has three hearts you expect him to bid 3♡. With a spade stopper, he can bid 3NT. Without either a spade stopper or three hearts, he will probably try a Fourth Suit Forcing 3♠ just to see what you do next!

5.

♠ K65
♥ AQ1054
♦ 542
♣ 75

Recommended Bid: 3♥

At first sight, it is tempting to bid 3♠ to show your no trump stopper but in my view this would be a mistake. The problem with 3♠ is that it doesn't show five hearts, so bid 3♥ to make this clear. If partner needs help is spades, he will surely bid a Fourth Suit Forcing 3♠ to give you another chance to bid 3NT.

6.

♠ K75
♥ AJ42
♦ QJ5
♣ 75

Recommended Bid: 3NT

An easy one here, plenty enough values for game and stoppers in both unbid suits. Bid 3NT.

7.

♠ QJ5
♥ A853
♦ 9764
♣ 75

Recommended Bid: Pass

Of course, it is possible that you will make 3NT if you play in it, but there is no guarantee. With a minimum hand for responding 1♥, why should you feel that you have to make another bid.

7

THE SLAM ZONE

If you have turned to this chapter in the hope of finding an instant panacea to solve all your problems in the slam zone, you will probably be sorely disappointed. While it is true to say that much of this chapter is designed to improve the tools that may help you to make the final decision, I believe that, for most players, the real barrier to improving their slam bidding is recognising the combined potential of the two hands.

Unless the basic structure of your system is sound and you follow the principles expounded in the earlier parts of this book, you will have great difficulty distinguishing between hands where it is a sensible investment to venture above game to explore the slam possibilities, and hands where the chances of slam are so remote that the risk of going down at the five level outweighs the potential gain of bidding a slam. By increasing the degree of definition in your sequences up to the game level, you should be able to reduce the risk of proceeding to the five level on the wrong hand significantly, while identifying hands on which you can explore that little bit further without passing your safety level.

Perhaps an example will help to illustrate exactly what I mean. Your partner opens 1♡, and you respond 1♠ looking at:

♠ A10876
♡ 75
♢ AQ65
♣ 86

Rather to your surprise, your partner leaps to 4♠, and it is up to you! However, you look at it, this is a pretty good hand and with partner having in the region of seventeen points with four card spade support, it is tempting to press on with 5♢ – but, in my view, if you trust your partner, you should pass. Why?

Well, would you blame your partner for raising to game with something like:

♠ KJ53
♡ AKQJ4
◇ K5
♣ 92

Over your 5◇, dependent on your style, he will either bid 5♠ directly, or 5♡, in which case he would pass your 5♠ bid as he doesn't have a club control. All very reasonable, except that after you have lost the first two club tricks you will need to guess the location of the spade queen right to make your contract. No matter how strong the vibes are, sometimes you will get it wrong.

Of course, you can claim that you were unlucky, and indeed in many ways you were. You were unlucky that partner's trumps weren't that bit better and you were unlucky that you failed to consider what alternative bids partner might have made instead of raising directly to 4♠.

Let's give partner nearly perfect cards, something along the lines of:

♠ KQ53
♡ AKQ42
◇ 75
♣ A2

Now, 6♠ is excellent, but in all honesty your partner can't have that hand for he would have made an advance cuebid of 4♣ and not just raised you to 4♠. Alter the hand so that opener has a singleton in either minor and most of the hands that would make the slam good would also qualify for a jump to 4♣ or 4◇. In fact, about the only way that partner can have enough to make the slam a good prospect without him being good enough to make a jump cuebid is if his hand includes the ◇K and the ♣A, when your ◇Q will provide a parking place for his losing club. Even then, he will need to have relatively weak hearts and good spades, something like:

♠ KQJ3
♡ A8542
◇ K5
♣ A6

and many expert players would still jump to 4♣ with this. Remove the ♠J and the slam is nowhere near as attractive a contract.

Without any doubt, one of the great skills of bidding is to bear in mind not only the bids that your partner actually made, but also those that he might have made, but didn't.

Cuebidding

You open 1♠ and you hear your partner raise to 3♠, how do you proceed holding:

♠ KQ7642
♡ AKJ4
♢ 75
♣ A

With partner showing four card spade support and about ten high card points, you will probably be feeling quite bullish, but unless your partner has at least second round control in diamonds you would certainly not want to get too high. In this situation the normal approach is to bid 4♣, a cuebid showing control in clubs. The idea is to find out if your partner can show a control in diamonds by cuebidding 4♢.

If partner owns the ♢A he is likely to cuebid 4♢, but what are you going to do if he just bids 4♠? Could your partner still have such a highly suitable hand as:

♠ A983
♡ 76
♢ KQ6
♣ J752

when 6♠ is certainly an excellent contract?

In my view, even if you are a firm believer that a cuebid should normally show first round control, the answer should be no! Why is this?

The normal argument for refusing to cuebid a second round control in this type of situation is that 'Partner will think I have the ace and so he may get too high'. This is a totally fallacious position to adopt with this hand. Even though you do not have the ace of diamonds, you have adequate compensation in that you hold the ace of trumps; a card which by its very nature you cannot show by cuebidding. Put it another way, if your partner jumps to slam expecting that you will put the ♢A down in the dummy, he is unlikely to be disappointed when you produce the ♠A instead!

At the very least, if I can persuade the most conservative player that he should cuebid 4♢ with this hand, it will take a lot of pressure off his partner to make more than one slam try on the opening hand under discussion.

Once I persuade you that you really ought to cuebid with this hand it becomes totally clear that, in the absence of a 4♢ cuebid from responder, opener should not proceed above 4♠.

Let's continue the discussion by asking you how you would plan your campaign with the following hand:

> ♠ AQ754
> ♡ AKQ4
> ◇ Q75
> ♣ 5

Once again, you open 1♠ and partner raises to 3♠, what are you going to bid now?

Once again, you have a good hand and the traditional cuebidders might well issue a slam try by cuebidding 4♡. No doubt, they would expect their partner to cooperate by cuebidding 5◇ if he had a suitable hand such as:

> (a)   ♠ K982
> ♡ 62
> ◇ AK42
> ♣ 982

when 6♠ is virtually laydown but they would be most aggravated if he had the audacity to cuebid 5♣ on:

> (b)   ♠ K982
> ♡ 62
> ◇ 982
> ♣ AK42

when even 5♠ should go down. Obviously, apart from the switch round in the minors, hands (a) and (b) are identical, so how is responder to know which one is gold dust and which one is rhubarb?

To me, it is perfectly clear that opener should issue a slam try, but he should bid 4♣ and not the space-consuming 4♡. Admittedly, you do not have the ♣A or a void in clubs but you do have compensating top controls in the majors. If you cuebid 4♣ and partner bids 4♠ (which he would be forced to do with hand (b)) you should be 100% confident that you do not have a slam on. Obviously, responder would cuebid 4◇ with hand (a) but in addition he should also cuebid 4◇ whenever he has second round control, providing he has a compensating first round control. In this case, as you hold the ♠A, it would have to be the ♣A.

Blackwood

As you will know Blackwood is the use of a bid of 4NT to ask for the number of aces partner holds. The responses follow the easy scheme that:

> 5♣ shows 0 or 4 aces
> 5◊ shows 1 ace
> 5♡ shows 2 aces
> 5♠ shows 3 aces

What is not quite so obvious is that Blackwood is principally a convention designed to keep you out of a slam missing two aces. The idea is that you should have already established that you intend to bid a slam before you use the convention. In other words, if you find that you are missing only one ace you are expected to be bidding a small slam. In particular, this means that before using Blackwood you should have a good expectation that you have all the suits controlled. Let's look at an example:

(a)   ♠ AQ9764
     ♡ AKQ42
     ◊ 5
     ♣ 7

(b)   ♠ KQ964
     ♡ AKQ53
     ◊ 75
     ♣ A

Once again, let's suppose that the auction starts with 1♠ from you, raised to 3♠ by partner. Both hands have enormous potential, and hand (a) is particularly suitable for Blackwood. If partner has no aces you would clearly settle for 5♠; if he has one ace you would bid 6♠, expecting that at worst it would depend on a spade guess; and, if he has two aces, you might just employ some further gadget to find out if he has the king of trumps before deciding whether to settle for just 6♠ or trying for a grand slam.

Hand (b) is nowhere near as suitable. If partner has no aces you will hope that 5♠ is not too high, and if he has two aces you should probably take a shot at the grand slam – which should have good play unless his red suit distribution is highly unfavourable. But what are you going to do if he only has one ace?

Obviously, partner could hold the ♠A and the ◊KQ, or the ◊AK when you would clearly want to be in 6♠; but equally he could hold the ♠A and the ♣KQ, in which case you are likely to lose two diamond tricks if you play in the slam. How do you find out? Certainly not by using Blackwood.

Cuebid 4♣ and, if partner cooperates by bidding 4◊, you can use Blackwood then in some safety.

Over the years there have been all sorts of variations made in the use of 4NT as an ace-asking convention. Names that immediately spring to mind are the Culbertson 4-5 convention, Norman and both Byzantine and Roman Blackwood. However, unless you are in the process of forming a long-running partnership with substantial international ambitions, it is my view that none of these conventions has sufficient merit to warrant the additional memory effort required to learn and use them effectively.

However, I would confess to having a very different view of Roman Key Card Blackwood which seems to be all the rage with most expert players these days.

Roman Keycard Blackwood (RKCB)

The basis of Roman Keycard is that the king of trumps is regarded as a fifth ace. The additional feature is that possession of the trump queen or lack of it is also identified quickly. The basic responses to 4NT are:

$5\clubsuit$ = 0 or 3 out of five
$5\diamondsuit$ = 1 or 4 out of five
$5\heartsuit$ = 2 or 5 without the trump queen
$5\spadesuit$ = 2 or 5 with the trump queen

Then, after the $5\clubsuit$ and $5\diamondsuit$ responses, if the 4NT bidder wants to know about the queen of trumps, he can use the next step up (excluding the trump suit) as a relay to find out.

So, suppose that you pick up this collection:

$\spadesuit$ J742
$\heartsuit$ AK
$\diamondsuit$ KQJ65
$\clubsuit$ A5

and hear partner open $1\spadesuit$. Obviously there is a case to go slowly but, with controls in all the outside suits and a good source of tricks on the side, it is tempting to launch into Blackwood immediately. So playing Keycard the auction starts:

$1\spadesuit$	4NT
$5\clubsuit$	$5\diamondsuit$
?	

Notice that, while we have yet to support spades, on this type of direct sequence it is clear that spades must be regarded as the trump suit. Thus, in calculating how many aces he has, the opener will have to count the $\spadesuit$K as an ace.

So we've already asked for aces and have found out that partner has zero or three out of five, and it would be a very bizarre hand if he actually had zero. So we know that partner has the ♠AK and the ◇A. Now, we ask for the queen of trumps by bidding 5◇.

How does the responder to Blackwood show whether he has the queen of trumps or not? At this stage opinions differ. However, in my view, it makes most sense to use the next step up to deny the queen of trumps. Then, any other bid shows the trump queen.

So, on our example hand, if partner bids anything other than 5♡ over 5◇ he must have the spade queen, and we can bid the grand slam in comfort.

But what if he doesn't have the queen of trumps but he does have a six card spade suit? Now, despite missing the queen, we would still want to be in 7♠.

Curiously enough, this really shouldn't be a problem for Acol players on this sequence. When we jumped to 4NT it was quite clear that spades were agreed as trumps immediately and, as the opener only guaranteed holding four spades when he opened 1♠, it should be clear to him that the 4NT response also showed four spades. Once the opener can be reasonably sure that his partner has four card support then, when responder asks him for the trump queen, if he holds AKxxxx he should use his judgement to say, yes he has it.

If the 4NT bidder continues with 5NT at any stage, he is guaranteeing that you have all the aces between you and inviting you to show any additional tricks that you might have.

Suppose you hold:

♠ KQ765
♡ A5
◇ KQJ10
♣ 76

You open 1♠ and partner responds 3♣. You bid 3◇ and your partner bids 3♠. As it is most unlikely that partner has jumped the bidding on a queen high suit, you could use RKCB yourself if you really wanted to but you show unusual restraint by cuebidding 4♡. Partner takes control now by using RKCB himself. Over 4NT you respond 5♠ which shows possession of two out of five 'aces' plus the queen of trumps, and partner then bids 5NT – what would you bid next?

Clearly partner is looking for a grand slam, and showing that he has the other three aces, so you know that you actually have three extra diamond tricks. So, grasp the bull by the horns and bid the grand slam. The full deal turns out to be:

As you can see there is no problem in 7♠ unless spades break 4-0.

Some of my pupils have objected to this hand on the basis that, if partner was looking for the ♣K when he bid 5NT, he might be sorely disappointed but in my view they are ignoring an important principle of constructive bidding. If you held:

♠ KQ765
♡ A5
◇ K765
♣ K6

what should you bid, after the auction has started:

1♠	3♣
3◇	3♠
?	

At the stage, where we bid 4♡ in the previous auction, if we decide to cuebid rather than leap into Blackwood, 4♣ is certainly the right bid. Why?

Very simply, partner has jumped in this suit and possession of the ♣K is likely to make a very great difference to his assessment of the combined playing strength of the two hands. Just consider how important the ♣K is if partner's holding is something like ♣AQJ54.

Raises to the Five Level

Have you ever considered what the following sequences mean?

(a)	1♠	3♠		(b)	1♠	3♠
	4◇	4♡			4♣	4◇
	5♠				4♡	4♠
					5♠	

In both sequences the opener has pressed on to 5♠, but the two 5♠ bids have totally different meanings.

Let's look at each sequence in turn:

On sequence (a), opener has cuebid in diamonds, heard a return cuebid in hearts and then jumped to 5♠. What is he doing?

The traditional interpretation of this sequence is that the opener is asking for a club control. Think about it! If opener had a club control, he would have either bid 4♣ two rounds earlier or he could bid 5♣ instead of 5♠ now. So, when there is one unbid suit, a jump to the five level in a major has come to be a request for partner to bid on to slam with a control in the unbid suit.

For the example sequence we are considering, the opener might have:

> ♠ AK7643
> ♡ 5
> ◇ AKQ5
> ♣ 75

Now let's consider sequence (b). This time opener has cuebid in both clubs and hearts, while responder has made a return cuebid in diamonds before signing off in 4♠. So what does this raise to 5♠ mean?

This time, opener is asking the responder for good trumps. He might have:

> ♠ K6543
> ♡ A
> ◇ K3
> ♣ AKQ52

Expecting his partner to have the ◇A, opener wishes to play in slam providing responder has reasonable trumps, say ♠QJxx or better.

Now, before giving you the opportunity to test out these slam bidding tools, there is another area of bidding where playing standard methods, average players tend to get notoriously bad results. Of course, I refer to the Acol 2♣ opening, or more specifically the standard methods of responding to it. The discussion is included here because of the frequency of sequences that start with a 2♣ opening ending up in the Slam Zone.

Opening 2♣

Unfortunately you don't pick up hands strong enough to open 2♣ very often but, when you do, how often do you end up in a silly contract? Part of the reason for inefficiency in this area is a general lack of experience as to the best way to proceed but the main influence is the unwieldy methods that normal Acol recommends in this area.

The general approach requires that responder has one and half honour tricks before he gives a positive response to a 2♣ opening, that is an ace and a king, three kings or a king/queen and a king; otherwise with the possible exception of a 2NT response he has to bid 2♢.

This has the effect of making responses other than 2♢ incredibly rare and it puts a lot of strain on the structure of bidding after the 2♢ response. As the 2NT rebid after a 2♢ response is non-forcing, the popular treatment of any balanced 25-26 count is to jump to 3NT on the second round of the bidding. While it makes sense to bid over this using the same general treatments that you might use over a 2NT rebid, the auction is already uncomfortably high. All in all, a rather silly approach on a selection of hands which have enormous slam-going potential.

In the early 1980s, a group of English players including the likes of Tony Forrester, Raymond Brock and Brian Senior experimented with a totally different style of responding to 2♣. The idea was that all positive hands should respond 2♢, 2♡ was reserved for all hands with about 0-4 points and balanced hands in the 5-7 point range, while the other bids were used to deal with hands with a five card suit in the 5-7 point range. Certainly, it seemed to me that this was a step in right direction but there is so much work involved in sorting out the fine tuning that such methods are unlikely to come into common usage.

For most fairly regular, but not too serious partnerships, let me make an alternative suggestion. Why not play the responses to 2♣ to show how many aces and kings the responding hand has in simple ascending order? For some years I have experimented with using this scheme:

$$2♢ = 0 \text{ controls (i.e. no ace or king)}$$
$$2♡ = 1 \text{ control (i.e. one king)}$$
$$2♠ = 2 \text{ controls (i.e. one ace or two kings)}$$
$$2NT = 3 \text{ controls (i.e. one ace and one king, or three kings)}$$
and so on.

Bids of 3♡ and higher could sensibly be used for other meanings as the chance of you ever having six controls facing a genuine 2♣ opening is very small indeed.

Obviously this scheme of things has the great merit of being very easy to learn, but is there anything to be gained by adopting it?

There is one obvious advantage and one that is somewhat less obvious. Let's start with the more obvious one, which is simply that there is a whole range of hands where being told just how many aces and kings partner holds can be very useful. Let's look at one or two examples:

Suppose you pick up a hand like:

You open 2♣ and hear partner bid:

(a) 2◇ denying a single control

Your ambition is immediately limited to determining whether you are going to play in 4♠ or 3NT. Your likely plan will be to bid your spades and then rebid 3NT.

(b) 2♡ showing one control

As partner must have one of the red kings, you know immediately that 4♠ is safe. Your effort here will be to try and find out if partner has a reasonable suit of his own, as you have potential to make a slam in any of the other three suits. If the auction were to proceed something like:

2♣	2♡
2♠	3♣
3♠	4♣
?	

wouldn't you be thinking of playing in 6♣. Note that if you had rebid 3NT, in all probability partner would pass with ♣J10xxxx and the ◇K, yet 6♣ looks excellent.

Of course, partner might have the ♡K and not the diamond king and then 6♣ would not be so good on a diamond lead. However, note that you can find out by bidding 4◇ yourself. If partner has the ♡K he will surely bid 4♡, and you will settle for 4♠; if he has the ◇K he will bid something else and you can bid 6♣ with some confidence.

(c) 2♠ showing two controls

Ironically you would now much prefer him to have both kings rather than the ♣A, but at least you can already be certain of ten tricks.

(d) 2NT showing three controls

Now you already know that he has the ♣A and a red king. If its the ◇K you might have to settle for just twelve tricks but, if you find out that he has the ♡K instead, the grand slam should make barring ridiculous distributions.

As you can see, knowing how many controls partner has gives you a good idea of the range of possible contracts very early in the proceedings.

What about the second advantage? Consider, a more balanced hand, such as:

♠ AQJ4
♡ KQ94
◇ AQ4
♣ AK

the sort of hand that is all too regularly bid 2♣ – 2◇ – 3NT. Now, even adopting our new methods, we are in a similar position if partner responds 2◇ to our 2♣ opening, though my own preference would be to try 2♡ at this stage rather than 3NT. However, there are many responding hands that would have formerly been 'negative' responses that will now respond 2♡ or even 2♠. In both of those situations it should be clear that a 2NT will now be forcing, which will allow the bidding to proceed at a conveniently lower level.

The opposite side of this coin means that with a hand like:

♠ K5
♡ A4
◇ K5
♣ AKQ7652

I can start by opening 2♣ and if I get a response showing less than three controls I can simply gamble out 3NT.

I am not trying to suggest that this change in method will be a panacea for all ills, but I do believe that many players would find it well worth a try.

THE SLAM ZONE: QUIZ 1

It is all very well deciding to play Roman Keycard Blackwood but in practice far too many disasters occur because the players disagree as to whether a bid is Blackwood or not. Certainly, in some casual partnerships I have agreed with my partner that 4NT is always Blackwood unless or until we have specifically agreed that it isn't. At least in this text, we don't have to address the different ways in which 4NT might be used in a competitive sequence, but even so, it is well worth making sure that you are on the same wavelength as your partner in the more common 4NT situations.

So, this is a quiz with a difference. All you have to do is decide in each of the following sequences: what does 4NT mean?

1. 1NT   4NT

2. 1NT   3♡
   4♣   4NT

3. 2NT   3◇ (Transfer)
   3♡   4NT

4. 1♡   4NT

5. 1♠   3♠
   4♣   4♡
   4NT

6. 1♠   2♣
   2◇   4NT

7. 1♠   2◇
   3♣   4NT

8. 1♠   3◇
   3♡   4◇
   4NT

ANSWERS TO THE SLAM ZONE: QUIZ I

In each of the following sequences: what does 4NT mean?

1.   1NT   4NT

We start with a situation where nearly all players are agreed that 4NT should be natural and invitational (and if you want to ask for aces you might use 4♣, Gerber). However, while that may be clear, it is nowhere near so certain if you introduce a Stayman response first. For example, suppose the bidding starts:

                                    1NT   2♣
                                    2♠   4NT

Is this Blackwood with spades agreed, or is it a balanced invitational strength hand with four hearts? My own inclination would be to the latter description but only because I would expect to be able to make a suitable advance cuebid in a minor on any hand where I might subsequently want to use Blackwood. If you play regularly with one player, do you know what your partner would mean if he bid this way?

2.   1NT   3♡
                                    4♣   4NT

Now, what is going on here? Presumably the responder is showing a forcing hand with hearts and opener's 4♣ bid is a cuebid showing heart support, a club control and a maximum. As hearts are clearly agreed as trumps, 4NT must be Blackwood.

3.   2NT   3◇ (Transfer)
                                    3♡   4NT

This sequence is totally different. By transferring into hearts and then bidding 4NT, responder is showing a five card heart suit in a balanced hand with slam invitational values. Except by special agreement this is not Blackwood.

4.   1♡   4NT

Here, 4NT is Blackwood with hearts agreed by inference. Indeed, in this situation it is difficult to think of any sensible alternative meaning.

5.

1♠	3♠
4♣	4♡
4NT	

Another clearcut sequence with spades agreed from the off. To me, it is quite clear that 4NT should be Blackwood especially given a fairly free-wheeling style of cuebidding. However, I could introduce you to quite a few internationals who would prefer to play this as a quaint form of cuebid, maybe showing a further heart control. Frankly, for 99.9% of players, it is not worth looking further than Blackwood.

6.

1♠	2♣
2◊	4NT

On this sequence there is probably enough room for responder to develop his hand with either a natural type or a hand with four card diamond support as, if need be, he can toil through Fourth Suit Forcing. Having said that, most players would suggest that this should be Blackwood with opener's last bid suit, diamonds, agreed by inference.

7.

1♠	2◊
3♣	4NT

This one is as clear as mud. To me it seems obvious that 4NT should be natural and invitational. The sequence has already arrived at the three level, so there is insufficient space to develop and describe the responding hand. What are you supposed to do with a hand that feels too good for 3NT but not strong enough to sensibly try 6NT. Meanwhile, if instead you have the luxury of having four card club support you can proceed by raising to 4♣. Remember that partner's 3♣ bid was forcing to game.

8.

1♠	3◊
3♡	4◊
4NT	

Finally, an interesting one. Responder has shown a very good hand with a solid or near solid diamond suit.and is inviting opener to cuebid. So, what is opener supposed to do with a 5-4-1-3 minimum hand with a club stopper other than bid 4NT?

THE SLAM ZONE: QUIZ II

First, let's take a look at the opener's hand.
What would you do in each of the following situations?

1. ♠ KQ8763
    ♡ 5
    ◇ AKQ54
    ♣ 8

1♠	3♠
?	

2. ♠ KQ6432
    ♡ J53
    ◇ A5
    ♣ 75

1♠	3♣
3♠	4♡
4♠	5♠
?	

3. ♠ KQ5
    ♡ AKJ432
    ◇ A
    ♣ 842

1♡	3♡
?	

4. ♠ AK654
    ♡ AJ52
    ◇ 75
    ♣ K5

1♠	2♣
2♡	4◇
?	

5. ♠ AQ1054
    ♡ 64
    ◇ QJ54
    ♣ A5

1♠	2♡
2♠	3◇
?	

6. ♠ K5
    ♡ AK642
    ◇ J53
    ♣ AK5

1♡	1♠
2NT	3♡
?	

7. ♠ AJ642
    ♡ Q742
    ◇ K4
    ♣ A5

1♠	2◇
2♡	4NT
5♠	5NT
?	

8. ♠ AKQJ5
    ♡ K52
    ◇ 753
    ♣ Q7

1♠	3♣
3♠	3NT
4♣	4◇
?	

ANSWERS TO THE SLAM ZONE: QUIZ II

What would you do in each of the following situations?

1.
♠ KQ8763
♡ 5
◇ AKQ54
♣ 8

1♠	3♠
?	

Recommended Bid: 4◇

It is sorely tempting to blast into 4NT planning to bid 6♠ if partner shows two aces, and settling for 5♠ if he only has one. However, it is not clear how you explain your choice of action when partner's hand is:

♠ J952
♡ KQ42
◇ 72
♣ KQ5

With eleven high card points and four card support you can barely blame him for raising you to 3♠. Curb your impetuosity and cuebid 4◇ and hope that with two aces partner is tempted into some forward move.

2.
♠ KQ6432
♡ J53
◇ A5
♣ 75

1♠	3♣
3♠	4♡
4♠	5♠
?	

Recommended Bid: 6◇

This is a command sequence. Partner's 5♠ demands that you bid on to slam with any diamond control. With the king or a singleton, you should just bid the slam but with the ace you should cuebid it just in case partner is planning to bid a grand slam. Strangely enough, although you had very much a minimum opening bid, your hand has rapidly gained in stature. Now, if partner put me to the test by bidding 6♡ over 6◇, I would happily bid the grand slam in spades.

3.
                                      ♠ KQ5
                                      ♡ AKJ432
                                      ◇ A
                                      ♣ 842

                            1♡   3♡
                            ?

Recommended Bid: 3♠

Slam prospects on this hand largely depend on partner having a good club
holding and little, if anything, wasted in diamonds. Bid 3♠ to leave space
for partner to cuebid 4♣. If he does you can continue with 4◇.

4.   ♠ AK654
                                      ♡ AJ52
                                      ◇ 75
                                      ♣ K5

                            1♠   2♣
                            2♡   4◇
                            ?

Recommended Bid: 4NT

What is going on here? Partner's jump to 4◇ is a cuebid agreeing hearts as
trumps. While you only have fourteen high card points you really do have
an excellent hand with excellent controls and what may prove to be the
vital ♣K in partner's suit. Playing ordinary Blackwood, 4NT would not
really help you very much, but RKCB gives you the opportunity to find out
about the king and queen of trumps as well, so it's well-suited for this hand.

5.   ♠ AQ1054
                                      ♡ 64
                                      ◇ QJ54
                                      ♣ A5

                            1♠   2♡
                            2♠   3◇
                            ?

Recommended Bid:4♣

As you have the ♣A you could bid 3NT here, however your cards look
excellent for playing in diamonds. The low diamond honours will fill part-

ner's suit admirably; indeed you have such good cards for diamonds that it is not that difficult to construct a hand where a diamond contract would be best, even if turns out to be only a 4-3 fit. So it looks right to support diamonds, but we might as well take the opportunity to cuebid 4♣ on the way. Clearly this should show a good raise in diamonds with club control, limited by the fact that you rebid 2♠, and that is what you've got.

6.
        ♠ K5
        ♡ AK642
        ◇ J53
        ♣ AK5

1♡	1♠
2NT	3♡
?	

Recommended bid: 4♣

Partner's 3♡ is offering a choice between 4♡ and 3NT. As you have five hearts and rather poor diamonds, it is clear that you should prefer 4♡ but, with excellent high cards and a key card in partner's suit, take the opportunity to stress your suitability for hearts by cuebidding 4♣. Just occasionally, partner will have enough to be able to take advantage of this accurate description of your hand.

7.
        ♠ AJ642
        ♡ Q742
        ◇ K4
        ♣ A5

1♠	2◇
2♡	4NT (RKCB)
5♠	5NT
?	

Recommended bid: 6◇

Obviously your partner was pleased to hear your 2♡ rebid, as 4NT is Roman Keycard Blackwood with hearts as trumps. Your 5♠ response promised two out of the five aces plus the queen of hearts but now partner has bid 5NT to confirm that you have all the aces and ask you if you have anything extra. While you have given a fair description of your hand so far, you do have a very important card that partner doesn't know about yet, the ◇K. So bid 6◇ to identify this extra value.

8.   ♠ AKQJ5
                                         ♡ K52
                                         ◇ 753
                                         ♣ Q7

1♠	3♣
3♠	3NT
4♣	4◇
?	

Recommended bid: 4NT

You have followed a clever campaign so far. After the jump to 3♣ you had plenty in reserve for your 3♠ bid. When partner clarified his hand type by rebidding 3NT you made the clever forward move of supporting clubs. Now partner has cuebid in diamonds, you have sufficient cover to try RKCB with clubs agreed even though your final destination is likely to be 6♠.

THE SLAM ZONE: QUIZ III

This time, switch seats to take the responding hand:

1. ♠ J742
♡ 75
◇ KQ5
♣ A842

| 1♠ | 3♠ |
| 4♣ | ? |

2. ♠ Q1054
♡ KQ5
◇ K642
♣ 75

| 1♠ | 3♠ |
| 4♣ | ? |

3. ♠ Q742
♡ AJ65
◇ 75
♣ K65

1♠	3♠
4◇	4♡
5♠	?

4. ♠ J764
♡ AQ62
◇ K52
♣ J2

1♠	3♠
4◇	4♡
5♣	?

5. ♠ KQ6
♡ 74
◇ A632
♣ 7632

2♠	3♠
4♣	4◇
4♡	?

6. ♠ K65
♡ J754
◇ KQ
♣ 8542

2♠(Strong)?

7. ♠ 82
♡ KQ87
◇ A6
♣ A9742

1♠	2♣
2♡	4◇
4NT	5♣
5◇	?

8. ♠ AJ5
♡ 542
◇ AK642
♣ A6

| 1♠ | 3◇ |
| 3♠ | ? |

ANSWERS TO THE SLAM ZONE: QUIZ III

This time, switch seats to take the responding hand:

1.

♠ J742
♡ 75
◇ KQ5
♣ A842

1♠	3♠
4♣	?

Recommended Bid: 4◇

There is nothing to be afraid of here. You can afford to cuebid 4◇ because you have the compensating ♣A.

2.

♠ Q1054
♡ KQ5
◇ K642
♣ 75

1♠	3♠
4♣	?

Recommended bid: 4♠

With a very ordinary hand for the initial raise to 3♠ and no ace, cooperating by cuebidding 4◇ is a bit rich for me. Settle for 4♠ on the basis that you can own up to possession of the ◇K if partner does press on.

3.

♠ Q742
♡ AJ65
◇ 75
♣ K65

1♠	3♠
4◇	4♡
5♠	?

Recommended bid: 6♠

Partner has highlighted the lack of club control. You have one, so you should press on with 6♠.

4.
      ♠ J764
      ♡ AQ62
      ◇ K52
      ♣ J2

1♠	3♠
4◇	4♡
5♣	?

Recommended Bid: 5◇

Partner's 5♣ bid almost invites you to show a diamond feature if you have one. You should cuebid the ◇K now.

5.
      ♠ KQ6
      ♡ 74
      ◇ A632
      ♣ 7632

2♠ (Strong)	3♠
4♣	4◇
4♡	?

Recommended Bid: 5♠

You have shown support for spades and you have cuebid 4◇, but you could have less suitable cards for your initial raise to 3♠. Get the plus values of your hand off your chest now by jumping to 5♠.

6.
      ♠ K65
      ♡ J754
      ◇ KQ
      ♣ 8542

2♠	?

Recommended Bid: 5♠

While we are on the subject of strong twos, what would you respond with this hand? There are some old-fashioned textbooks which would claim that the immediate spade raise guarantees an ace; however, can anyone see a more sensible bid than 3♠ on this deal?

7.
<pre>
                    ♠ 82
                    ♡ KQ87
                    ◇ A6
                    ♣ A9742

        1♠   2♣
        2♡   4◇
        4NT   5♣
        5◇   ?
</pre>

Recommended bid: 6♡

Partner is now checking on whether you hold the queen of hearts. As you do, you must respond positively but with nothing extra to add simply sign off in 6♡.

8.
<pre>
                    ♠ AJ5
                    ♡ 542
                    ◇ AK642
                    ♣ A6

        1♠   3◇
        3♠   ?
</pre>

Recommended bid: 4♣

So you've already forced by jumping to 3◇ with this hand. When partner rebids his spades, cuebid 4♣ to show your club control on the way to 4♠.

By its very nature slam bidding is a vast subject, and there is no way of doing more than introducing the subject in the space available in this book. Hopefully, setting your course in the right direction will prove to be good start.

Overall, now that you have come to the end of this book, I think that you will agree that we have actually covered quite a lot of ground. However, the real test will only come after you have assimilated most of the ideas that I have put forward, and then put them into practice at the bridge table. Only then, as you watch your scores improve, will you really know that you are making progress. Good luck.